How to Create Alternative, Magnet, and Charter Schools That Work

Robert D. Barr and William H. Parrett

National Educational Service

Bloomington, Indiana   1997

Cover design by Bill Dillon

Printed in the United States of America

Printed on recycled paper

ISBN 1-879639-48-3

Contents

Acknowledgments v

About the Authors ix

Preface xi

Chapter 1
Times of Trouble, Visions of Hope 1

Chapter 2
Schools That Work 11

Chapter 3
Why Alternative Schools Are So Effective 27

Chapter 4
Established Alternative School Models 57

Chapter 5
Starting Alternative Schools 83

Chapter 6
Magnet Schools 109

Chapter 7
    Charter Schools 135

Chapter 8
    Alternative Schools: Solutions for Lasting Reform 171

Appendix I
    Frequently Asked Questions Regarding Alternative
    Schools 179

Appendix II
    Alternative Schools Research-Based Evaluation
    Criteria 187

Appendix III
    Alternative School Support Organizations 193

Appendix IV
    Sample Alternative Schools and Programs 203

Appendix V
    Sample Charter Schools 221

Appendix VI
    Charter School Support Contacts 227

Acknowledgments

WE HAVE MANY TO THANK for assistance in the research and writing of this book. First and foremost, our heartfelt gratitude goes out to the students, teachers, administrators, and parents who for over three decades have participated in, supported, and embraced alternative schools as a viable method for educating thousands of America's youth. Our sincere appreciation is extended to the communities, school boards, businesses, various agencies of state and local government, and others who have worked so hard to ensure the success of this concept.

We wish to acknowledge and thank several of those individuals who have conducted and guided much of the research and documentation on alternative schools over the past 30 years. The co-founders of the Indiana University Consortium on Options in Public Education, Vernon Smith and Daniel Burke, along with the late Mario Fantini and Martha Ellison, as well as Wayne Jennings, Nate Blackman, Joe Nathan, and Mary

Anne Raywid were all leaders and pioneers in the early days of alternative education.

We have relied substantially on the accomplishments of seasoned practitioners who have developed and operated those exemplary alternative programs that have become the models for practice. They include such individuals as Patricia Bolanos, Faye Bryant, Daniel Diedrich, Paul Erickson, Russ Harmelink, Michael Harris, Jerri Hartsock, Jay Hill, Nate Jones, Paula Kinney, Arnie Langberg, Rick Lear, Deborah Meier, Bob Farris, Al Narvaez, Gary Phillips, Diane Porter, Marian Pritchett, Marilyn Reynolds, Jim Rooney, Phil Schlemmer, Barbara Shoup, Freddi Jo Stevens, Mary Ellen Sweeney, Walter Smith, Bob Stark, Scott Williams, and Jan Zulich. We thank each of you and those we have inadvertently missed, for all you have done for the concept and this project.

Our work has benefited greatly from the diligent scholarship and published efforts of many colleagues. Individuals including Terrence Deal, Nolan Estes, Adam Gamoran, Howard Gardner, Tom Gregory, Jonathan Kozol, Henry Levin, Jerry Mintz, Greg Smith, Jerry Smith, Donald Waldrip, Gary Wehlage, and Tim Young have contributed significantly to the development of alternative approaches to schooling. We thank you for your efforts.

Sincere appreciation goes to a number of individuals who provided careful and thoughtful reviews of early manuscripts which helped to improve and shape the character of this book. Serious critiques and suggestions from Holly Anderson, Arzell Ball, Robert Cole, Daniel Diedrich, Allan Glatthorn, Jerri Hartsock, Curtis Hayes, Raymond Morley, Hillery Motsinger, Glenn Potter, Marilyn Reynolds, Jay Smink, Robert Taylor, and Wenden Waite have clearly strengthened and polished this effort. In particular, we thank Joe Nathan for his insights and recommendations which improved our final manuscript. To the students of Teaching Youth at Risk, a graduate class taught on the campus of Boise State University in the Fall of 1996, our sincere gratitude for your thoughtful comments. Special thanks go to doctoral student Gloria Pumphrey, who eagerly conducted field work and edited early chapters, and to Gaye Bluthardt for her tireless research support through the conclusion of the project.

We wish to thank Boise State University and the University of Alaska–Fairbanks for the institutional support provided for the early drafting and development of manuscripts. The completion of this book was greatly assisted by a number of individuals in the research and production phases. The hard work and careful assistance from Myrna Avila, Howard Cloud, Holly Costa, Rose Crabtree, Kathy Hughes, Laura Krip, Ona Law, Ernie Manzie, Donna Moore, Glenn Olsen, Ernie Roberson, Virginia Tsu, Kim Williamson, Ann Winslow, Yin Jian Jun, and Jena Zier allowed us to complete this project. Furthermore, we wish to express our sincere appreciation to the National Educational Service team who have assisted us through the various stages of development and production. They include Alan Blankstein, Nancy Shin, Julia Hunt, Tim Spears, David Ruetschlin, Lauren Gottlieb, and Bill Dillon for all their help in the production of this work.

We are indebted and appreciative for the understanding and encouragement provided by our families. To our children, Bonny, Brady, Mia, and Jonathan, we send our love and thanks. Finally, and most important of all, were Beryl Barr and Ann Dehner, who endeavored through this two-year effort with their husbands, serving as supporters, critics, and editors of the various stages of our work.

About the Authors

THROUGHOUT THEIR CAREERS, Robert Barr and William Parrett have been immersed in alternative education. Together the authors have actively participated in the challenges of alternative education from the origins of the movement over 25 years ago.

On two occasions, Robert Barr debated alternative schools with William F. Buckley, Jr. on special features of the nationally televised *Firing Line* program. He was called as an expert witness in desegregation trials to explain the role that magnet schools could play in troubled communities, and he has provided testimony to congressional committees of the United States Congress regarding the positive impact of alternative schools on reducing violence in schools. He co-authored the first published articles about alternative education, the first Phi Delta Kappa fastback on alternative schools, and the first book to appear in America on alternative education. He also created and co-edited the first national alternative school newsletter,

Changing Schools, and prepared the first national directory of alternative schools. He has assisted school districts throughout the nation in their efforts to develop, expand, or improve the alternative schools in their communities. Currently, Barr serves as the Dean of the College of Education at Boise State University in Idaho.

William Parrett was one of the first individuals to complete a doctoral dissertation which focused on alternative public schools, and he was a member of the first group of students to gain a Master's Degree in Alternative Education at Indiana University (later returning to direct the program). Since that time, he has had first-hand experience as a teacher and principal of alternative schools, as a researcher, and as an author of numerous articles, curriculum projects, and books on teachers in small, rural, alternative schools. He has recently co-produced an internationally acclaimed documentary film portraying the nexus of education, culture, and community in a small mountain village of Hokkaido, Japan. Currently, Parrett serves on the faculty and directs the Center for School Improvement at Boise State University.

Preface

IN THE EARLY 1970S, PESSIMISM ABOUT PUBLIC EDUCATION was on the rise. Books like *Death at an Early Age, Our Children Are Dying,* and *Crisis in the Classroom* all predicted dire futures for our youth and our schools, feeding public dissatisfaction and spurring even greater inquiry into the faults and failings of public education.

To counter this grim outlook, a small group of professors and students at Indiana University hosted a conference to try to find public schools that were humane, caring, and effective. As discussions progressed among representatives of the 20 or so schools invited to the conference, it quickly became evident that alone and independent of one another, some of these schools were pioneering a very unusual set of ideas. Everyone was surprised that all of the students in these schools had volunteered to participate, that the curriculum at each of these schools had been specifically designed to address the needs of its students, and that each school emphasized community learning requirements and performance competencies. In uncovering these commonalities, the group assembled in Indiana had participated in an historic event—they had "discovered" alternative schools.

Once the unique features of these schools were identified, the Indiana University researchers mounted a national search to find out if there were other such schools in operation. With support from the Johnson Foundation, they identified over 250 public schools that fit the description, including schools that had been operating quietly in New York, Pennsylvania, Oregon, Minnesota, and California since the early 1970s. They established a newsletter, *Changing Schools,* as well as the International Consortium for Options in Public Education, which conducted hundreds of state and regional conferences in the following years and convened two international conferences. The Indiana University team developed the first definition of alternative schools, identified different types of alternative schools, published the initial directories of alternative schools, authored several of the first major publications regarding alternative public schools, and worked with the editors of the major educational journals to focus special issues on alternative public schools.

Indiana University quickly became the recognized center for scholars and educators who were interested in alternative schools. Participants from across the nation and around the world traveled to Bloomington, Indiana to study and attend the Annual International Conference on Alternative Schools—a gathering of minds which has continued to thrive, celebrating its 25th anniversary in 1995.

At the urging of leaders from alternative schools across the country, a Masters Degree program was started at Indiana University in 1972. The program was planned and developed by alternative school practitioners from throughout the United States and built around a year-long teaching internship in an alternative school to best prepare students to teach in the rapidly expanding numbers of alternative schools. This program—the Alternative Schools Teacher Education Program (ASTEP)—soon received a national award for Distinguished Achievement from the American Association of Colleges of Teacher Education for innovative and successful teacher education.

We have both been honored to act as directors of this program at different times (Robert Barr was the first director) and to have helped shape this crucial field of alternative schools research from its infancy when we were both at Indiana University almost 25 years ago.

Based on these decades of work with all kinds of alternative schools, we have written *How to Create Alternative, Magnet, and Charter Schools That Work* as both a design blueprint and a detailed reference volume for those seeking to create or improve a school of choice. It offers a thorough and comprehensive review of the history, research, and successes of alternative, magnet, and charter schools. We have tried to anticipate the questions, address the concerns, and provide the information and insight readers will need to act. Also included are dozens of personal vignettes, experiences, and quotes from field interviews with educators, students, and parents which vividly illustrate the world of alternative, magnet, and charter schools.

A WORD OF CHALLENGE

Chances are, if you are reading this book you are probably not *entirely* content with the school or district in which you teach, not *completely* happy with your children's education in your neighborhood school, or not satisfied that only *"many"* students enrolled in your district's secondary schools are succeeding. But even if you are completely content with the state of affairs in your district or with your children, we challenge you to read this book for the legions of our youth who are not receiving a stimulating, quality education. Although we in the United States and Canada have the capacity to provide a quality education to all, the institution of public education simply has not chosen to provide it consistently.

Alternative schools can change that choice. Since the early 1970s, alternative public schools have continued to grow, mature, and improve. They have significantly contributed to the national discussion regarding choice in education, been employed to help desegregate urban schools in almost every major city in America, provided unique, specialized programs for the motivated and talented, and been public education's most effective strategy in addressing the needs of at-risk youth. Alternative schools have improved the lives of teachers and students for over thirty years. Alternative schools are certainly no fad. They have survived, expanded, and flourished for the simple reason that they work.

But alternative schools are more than effective. These schools have a way of transforming the people who associate with them. Individuals who have spent their lives in public education are often stunned by their initial encounter with alternative education. Remarks from parents, students, and teachers reveal this powerful impact: "This alternative school was an answer to my prayers," "For the first time, school is working," and "This incredible school has changed my life." Alternative schools liberate constituents; they unleash imagination and foster commitment.

Three decades of research have documented that alternative public schools are among the most successful educational innovations ever tried. This book provides the rationale and the procedures needed to start and to improve alternative schools. Most important, this book offers both an invitation and a challenge to educators and communities to provide the effective, meaningful educational experiences deserved by all youth.

1

Times of Trouble, Visions of Hope

You could have never made me believe it. I had been a principal for 15 years and had thought I had seen it all. I considered myself a burned-out old war horse, tough and cynical. Then the damnedest thing happened. I decided to gear down a bit in preparation for retirement and took this really cushy job as principal of this small alternative school with about 150 of the little tough guys I had been working with every day at the high school. Then something remarkable happened. It's hard to explain. The school has not only transformed these kids . . . it has transformed me. I have learned what an enormous force a good school can be. My hope has been renewed, and I have forgotten about retiring.

Alternative School Principal,
Oregon

I hate to admit it . . . but I have surrendered. I have just given up. I know that I used to be a great teacher, but that is simply no longer true. In fact, I think if other teachers were honest, they would say exactly the same. Teaching has become impossible. Our classrooms are being overwhelmed with kids who won't learn and kids who are so far behind that I wonder how they could ever catch up. Do you have any idea how many little kids are taking Ritalin and how many of the really bright kids have left for private or home schools? It's so sad . . . . I feel like the army has simply pulled out and deserted, and here I am alone in the front-line trenches with this sad group of needy kids. I don't know what else to do. I have sent up the white flag. I surrender.

High School Teacher,
Michigan

PUBLIC EDUCATION IN THE UNITED STATES is in turmoil. People cannot agree on whether public education is getting better or worse, whether we have the finest public schools in the world or if our schools have placed us all at risk. Do mediocre student achievement scores reflect that teaching is poor or simply that more high-risk students are staying in school and taking the tests? Are our nation's schools responsible for the technological brilliance that has taken humans to the moon, or for the millions of dollars spent by American corporations in teaching basic skills to their employees?

While we may disagree about the reasons for it, millions of youth are dropping out or failing to succeed in U.S. public schools. The system is failing to educate perhaps 30% or more of the nation's youth.

Disenchantment with public education has led to a massive exodus by parents. Millions of parents have chosen parochial and private schools. Many other parents simply are forsaking public education for home schooling. Between 1984 and 1994 the number of students being home schooled in the United States grew from 15,000 to 350,000 (Jeub, 1994). Increasing numbers of citizens are demanding tuition tax credits and vouchers to help finance their departure from public education; and more than 20 privately funded organizations have established grant programs to provide tuition vouchers to low-income families, enabling their children to attend private schools (Walsh, 1996). Some urban districts have abandoned the education establishment and have privatized their public schools.

The public school student body is changing. More of them are poor; more are handicapped; more are students with English as a second language; more are teen parents; more are violent (Hodgkinson, 1993).

For generations, families and their children have been assigned to schools based on required neighborhood attendance boundaries. The problems with this tradition have been documented clearly in Jonathan Kozol's compelling study, *Savage Inequalities* (1991). These archaic practices continue to polarize public education into rich districts and poor districts, creating a structure of educational apartheid that destroys our goal of providing free and equal education to all.

A number of forces, however, have combined to create a remarkable opportunity. Currents of systemic change are sweeping through communities and legislatures across the nation. At last there is a chance to significantly change our schools.

For more than three decades, a quiet revolution has been occurring. Districts are creating and expanding alternative public schools; and these schools are, indeed, working. In these unique public schools, the teachers are positive and the students are engaged. The community is actively involved with these schools. Daily attendance is high, as are expectations for student achievement. Discipline referrals and suspensions are low or absent, and dropout rates are very low. Even the neighboring conventional schools appear to benefit when alternatives are created and supported.

AN EDUCATION SOLUTION THAT WORKS: ALTERNATIVE SCHOOLS

After 13 years of doing daily battle with many of my students over the basic routines necessary to teach a class of 28, I have begun to change my philosophy. I can't effectively teach them all. The system absolutely won't allow me to provide the time and support so many of them need to catch up, to get excited about learning. A third or more of my students really need a different structure. This high school really isn't for all students. And it's not their fault!

High School Teacher,
Washington

This little alternative school has changed my life. I knew all along what a positive impact the school was having on kids; but when I came here to teach, I just didn't anticipate what the school would do for me. It was like coming up for air from the bottom of a deep pond. To teach in a small school where students and teachers care for and respect one another and work hard for common goals has been so important. I feel my spirit has been resurrected. Really. My hope for the future is reborn. I love this school!

Alternative School Teacher,
New York

At a time when confidence in public education is at an all-time low, many will find it surprising that there is an educational approach that really works. It is an approach that works effectively to alleviate the majority of problems associated with public education today. Sound too good to be true? Believe it. The approach is known as alternative education.

Alternative schools have been studied carefully for the past three decades. These studies have clearly documented that parents enthusiastically support these schools, that teachers love to work in these schools, that students become engrossed in learning and have better attendance, that student attitudes toward school become much more positive, and that many of these students have begun to develop positive personal goals for the first time in their lives. Alternative schools represent the most promising approach to solving the complex problems facing public education today (Raywid, 1994).

SCHOOLS OF CHOICE

Everyone tried hard to believe that all schools were alike, that all teachers were alike, and that all students learned in the same way. Unfortunately, such an idea borders on the absurd. This idea would be like assembling a group of Roman Catholics, Jews, Pentecostals, Jehovah's Witnesses, Unitarians, Buddhists, Baptists, Muslims, and Methodists into a single building and calling it a "church." And if this "church" was modeled after public education, families would be "graduated" each year to a different religious faith to serve their needs.

Or what if health services were provided in the same way that we provide public education? It would be like grouping a general practitioner, a chiropractor, an osteopath, an acupuncturist, a Christian Scientist, a faith healer, an internist, and a surgeon into a building and calling it a health clinic. Each time a family returned to the clinic for services, they would be arbitrarily scheduled with a different medical practitioner. Could anything be more ridiculous?

To take a group of teachers with philosophies often as diverse as those in religion and medicine and place them into a single building and call the place a school is equally senseless. Yet this is precisely the rule of practice in public education today.

Professor,
Idaho

For a concept that has revolutionary implications for public education, the idea of alternative schools is really quite simple. Alternative education involves little more than diversifying public education by creating an array of educational programs designed to meet the needs of specific groups of students and providing those programs to parents, students, and teachers through voluntary choice. More recently, the concept of alternative education has come to mean replacing rules, regulations, and outdated course requirements with student performance outcomes.

The success of alternative schools has disproved the traditional idea that all schools must be alike and all teachers and students must teach and learn in the same manner. It has dramatized the failure of assigning students to schools based on where they live and has established performance as the standard of educational accountability. The acceptance and growth of alternative schools have potent implications for the future of public education in America. And while these implications have only begun to be realized, the potential effect is revolutionary.

Alternative educational programs recognize and respect the value of diversity. Alternative schools reflect the mounting evidence that supports multiple teaching and learning styles and diverse educational philosophies. They provide an effective, cost-conscious approach to diversifying public schools and providing focused educational programs to meet the widely differing needs of students, their parents, and their communities. This approach also provides a way to recognize, organize, and legitimize the diverse philosophical pathways to education.

The most startling phenomenon in public education today is the growing number of at-risk youth. Alternative schools represent the most effective approach to addressing the needs of these children. If students are behind in reading, alternative schools mobilize to ensure that reading is the focus of their program. If the students are pregnant or are teen parents, alternative schools provide health care, prenatal services, child care, and parenting classes. If students are far behind in basic skills, alternative schools provide an intensive approach so that students can accelerate their learning and catch up. Alternative schools offer relevant educational programs and attract students interested in particular, focused careers. Conventional public schools rarely can meet the needs of high-risk children and youth. Meeting the challenges of these youth is exactly what alternative schools have been designed to do.

Even if students stay in school and graduate—unless they are among the approximately 45% of youth who go on to higher education or technical training—they will find that they have learned few of the skills necessary to obtain an entry-level position with any promise of economic well-being. Eighty percent of jobs in the United States today demand skills in technology, yet the vast majority of public schools are only beginning to introduce computer technology into the curriculum. You still can find school vocational programs that teach typing and shorthand, carburetor repair, and how to properly set a dining table.

Alternative schools, especially magnet programs, have demonstrated that high schools can be developed with a curriculum that concentrates on such professions and job opportunities as aerospace studies, law and government, petrochemical engineering, media, international studies, health professions, and others. These schools have entered into partnerships with business and industry that include professional exchanges, student internships, and summer jobs prior to graduation. Alternative schools offer a way for districts to develop highly focused educational programs and attract students interested in particular careers.

Education researchers have known for more than 20 years that it is all but impossible to change an existing institution. All institutions are resistant to change, but this is even more true for schools. Not only do schools have the powerful constraint of tradition, but schools also are governed by a labyrinthine set of rules, regulations, and behavioral proprieties. Public schools create an institutional culture that changes the people who teach and learn in them. Most teachers and students ultimately will take on behaviors that reflect the particular culture of the school: work is conducted in 50-minute blocks, learning occurs at a desk with little interaction, teachers direct, students obey, etc. These cultural regularities and a host of others create a potent force that pressures those in schools to conform to common beliefs, norms, and expectations. New teachers do not change schools; schools change new teachers, causing them either to conform to the school culture or creating such frustration that they leave the profession after only a brief stay.

Existing schools can be changed, but it is a long, arduous process lasting at least five years. The process must involve intensive training and team building, new resources, community support, and consensus development. Success usually means that some teachers must be allowed to transfer to other schools.

A far easier, faster, and more enduring approach to school change is to create a new school and let parents, students, and teachers choose to participate. No other method of school reform has proven to be so efficient and effective. Seymour Sarason (1971), a noted scholar on the topic of school culture, has maintained for years that it is easier to start a new school than to attempt to change an established school.

If alternative schools had not been able to demonstrate significant gains, particularly with the students that conventional schools have been incapable of educating, it is likely that these schools would have disappeared from the education landscape. However, alternative schools have grown in number and respect because they have continued to demonstrate effectiveness, often with the most challenging students.

A growing number of states now require school districts to offer alternatives. Teachers love to teach in alternative schools. Parents seek them out for their children. And, perhaps most significant, students both achieve and give high praise for their experiences. Alternative schools will continue to proliferate for one simple reason: they work.

If a community is interested in starting, expanding, or improving educational alternatives, it is essential that the planning group learn from the years of research and experience that have accumulated. This research can point the way to developing a successful alternative school, whatever its specific program might be. The chapters that follow will examine this research and highlight the elements needed to develop a successful alternative school.

REFERENCES

Hodgkinson, H. (1993). American education: The good, the bad, and the task. In S. Elam (Ed.), *The state of the nation's public schools*. Bloomington, IN: Phi Delta Kappa.

Jeub, C. (1994). Why parents choose home schooling. *Educational Leadership, 52* (1), 50–52.

Kozol, J. (1991). *Savage inequalities: Children in America's schools*. New York: Harper Perennial.

Raywid, M.A. (1994). Alternative schools: The state of the art. *Educational Leadership, 52* (1), 26–31.

Sarason, S. (1971). *The culture of school and the problem of change*. Boston: Allyn & Bacon.

Walsh, M. (1996, March 20). Indianapolis study documents benefits of vouchers. *Education Week*, p. 3.

2

Schools That Work

People are always asking me, "What's so great about alternative schools?" For me, they are just a dream come true. I think you could travel throughout the country and talk to students, parents, and teachers in alternative schools and I bet you would hear a similar reaction. Anyone who has ever had the opportunity to teach or learn in an alternative school knows precisely what I'm speaking about: alternative schools create an environment where learning truly happens, where teachers love to teach, and where parents and students willingly participate. They work!

Past President,
Oregon Association of Alternative Schools

IMAGINE ENTERING A SCHOOL DISTRICT as a new parent and being presented with a menu of educational programs from which to select the most appropriate school for your child's developmental and educational needs. Imagine trained professionals welcoming and assisting you in determining which approach and program might best fit your child's needs. Imagine a district where bus transportation schedules did not dictate the daily schedule of educational offerings and where schools had extended programs that were open from 7:00 a.m. to 10:30 p.m. year round. Imagine a district philosophy of providing fair and equal access to education for all, backed up with the determination to graduate every student in the district. Reality or a dream? Unfortunately for most families and children, this is only a dream. Yet for the fortunate few in districts committed to alternative education, these dreams are reality and are available to every parent and child.

Alternative schools are the single most effective way to reform and improve public education that has ever been tried. This is true regardless of the form that the alternative school might take. It is true for schools within schools, for a single option serving a community, and for multiple magnet school offerings. It is true for alternatives that serve several school districts, and it is true for statewide residential schools that focus on such areas as math, science, and international studies. It also is true for the new alternative—charter schools.

The concept of developing "new" public schools that are designed to serve the needs of a particular group of students and their parents and offering these schools for voluntary participation has a remarkable 30-year track record of success. In an era when almost every attempt to reform, restructure, and improve public education has been met with disappointment, alternative schools stand alone in stark, positive contrast. Alternative schools work.

AN IMPRESSIVE TRACK RECORD

You never really know when you dream up a research project whether or not you will turn up anything

worthwhile. But we were reviewing all this positive research on alternative schools, and someone said that alternative schools really seemed to address the needs of kids. Then someone suggested, "Why don't we translate Maslow's Hierarchy of Needs into a survey and ask alternative school students and other public school students to complete a questionnaire," and the rest is history. I now hear people talking about this little survey as "landmark research." All we did was ask the right questions. Our findings were the most positive I have ever seen. I'm not sure what all goes on in alternative schools, but I can assure you of one thing—the students in these schools have a rock-solid belief that their "needs" are being met far better than other students we surveyed.

Professor,

Indiana University

No other effort at significantly changing schools has proven so effective so often, in so many different types of communities, with so many different types of students, as have alternative schools. In their various forms, alternative schools have been used effectively in transforming public school offerings in cities, suburbs, and small communities throughout the United States. They have been used to strengthen individual schools through the creation of schools within schools. They also have been used to redesign urban districts through the development of large numbers of magnet schools and programs. Alternative schools have been used to keep high-risk students in school, to attract dropouts back to school, and to teach these difficult students more effectively. They have been used to teach the gifted and talented. Alternative schools have been developed as traditional, back-to-basics schools and as highly flexible open schools. Alternative schools have used the Montessori approach and have been designed specifically for students with special talents in the performing arts. Perhaps most significant, in study after study, alternative schools have been shown to take students that more conventional public schools either could not or perhaps would not teach and have documented remarkable educational success (Barr & Parrett, 1995).

Originally, these schools were categorized by types of students (schools for dropouts, potential dropouts, gifted, etc.), curriculum focus (schools for performing and visual arts, science and math, environmental studies, world studies, etc.), or instructional emphasis (learning centers, schools without walls, individualized continuous progress, etc.). As thousands of alternative schools grew, scholars struggled to create an appropriate way to define and describe them.

Despite dramatic individual differences, the common characteristics of small settings, positive climate, choice of participation, a shared vision, focused curricula, program innovation, and high levels of student engagement, membership, and autonomy combine in alternative schools to create communities of support that are critical to the success of all students (Wehlage, Rutter, Smith, Lesko, & Fernandez, 1989).

Researchers have found that alternative schools can significantly improve student achievement. In comparative studies investigating the differences between alternative school students and those in other public schools, it has invariably been shown that alternative school students perform better. And in this violent age of guns, gangs, adolescent suicide, and Generation X cynicism, alternative school students are significantly less violent, have better school attendance, have a lower dropout rate, and have more positive attitudes than do most public school students. In numerous studies, alternative school students have been found to feel more connected with school than do other public school students. They feel better about themselves; they have more positive attitudes regarding teachers, learning, and schools; and they find that their basic human needs are being met better than are those of other public school students (Wehlage et al., 1989). In alternative schools a positive climate is the rule, not an exception.

Student achievement improves in alternative, magnet, and charter schools. In fact, few other educational approaches have documented such a direct, positive effect on student achievement. A number of studies over the past 30 years have documented that students in alternative, magnet, and charter schools learn better, achieve more, and have a higher standard of performance (Barr, 1981).

Students in alternative schools learn more than students in regular high schools and Catholic schools. In a recent study of 24,000 students in grades 8 through 12 and their test scores on national achievement tests administered at the 8th- and 10th-grade levels, researchers were surprised to discover that students in alternative magnet schools showed better achievement and higher scores than their counterparts in regular high schools as well as in Catholic schools. Even more impressive was the fact that the magnet schools enroll a larger percentage of poor and minority students (Gamoran, 1996).

In another study of 300 career academies (both stand-alone alternative schools and schools-within-schools), similar positive results regarding student achievement were documented (West, 1996).

Student attitudes improve since students' needs are met more effectively than in other public schools. In one of the classic research studies comparing students and teachers in alternative and conventional public schools, an impressive difference was discovered. Using Maslow's Hierarchy of Needs, students and teachers in a variety of alternative public schools reported that their "basic human needs" were much more fully satisfied than those of students in conventional schools.

The study looked at the top four levels of Maslow's Hierarchy of Needs (security, social, esteem, and self-actualization needs). At each level, alternative school teachers' and students' mean scores were higher than those of their conventional school counterparts. The researchers attributed the differences to freedom of choice rather than variations in school size, informality, and/or instructional approaches. They concluded that people were more likely to value—and feel satisfied by—a program that they chose, rather than by one that was imposed on them (Smith, Gregory, & Pugh, 1981).

An almost total lack of violence exists in alternative schools. Thirty years of research and congressional study have documented that there is little or no violence in alternative schools, even when students attending those schools have histories of violence and/or delinquency at other schools (Barr, 1981).

Alternative school students appear to be more successful in later life. Follow-up studies of selected public schools found that students who had attended alternative schools felt happier, more self-directed, and more personally effective; and they possessed more self-esteem than graduates of other schools' programs (Siebold & Jundson, 1996).

Today, alternative schools and their "offspring," magnet and charter schools, offer hope to the institution of public education. They provide this hope through choice, communities of support, positive results, and an ongoing, concerted effort to innovate, improve, and disseminate their successes.

INNOVATION, RESEARCH, AND DEVELOPMENT

On the fifth-grade achievement test, our daughter tested well over a year ahead of her age group. Of course we didn't need to see the test to know that. She always had been excited about learning but, unfortunately, had found most of her public schooling to be below her level and was often bored. She grew to dislike school and actively tried to not go. When we learned about a sixth-grade alternative program that would focus on the environment and emphasize the development of independent study skills, we immediately applied. The school was set up in two portable classroom buildings at the city zoo and was available to academically motivated sixth-grade kids from all over town. The teachers invited zoologists, biologists, and veterinarians to help teach the kids. The zoo and its grounds became the classroom. Our daughter, for the first time, "came alive" and was truly feeling challenged. She started doing independent projects and often wanted to visit the zoo on the weekends to check on the animals she was studying. Our daughter, after earning her degree in biology, is now working as a field biologist and continues to be as excited about her job as she was at the zoo.

Parent,

Grand Rapids, Michigan

Alternative schools have served as research and development centers for pioneering innovative practice in public education. It was in the St. Paul Open School that course graduation requirements were first successfully replaced with required learning competencies. It was in the Philadelphia Parkway School that researchers studying community learning experiences found that students could learn effectively outside of schools. Alternative schools pioneered in the development of focused curricula, multi-age grouping, cross-age tutoring, democratic school governance, and site-based management. Alternative schools developed year-round school calendars and semester, weekly, and daily schedules modeled after colleges and universities.

Recently, charter schools have demonstrated that once programs are exempted from state education regulations, they can create new and highly efficient approaches to school budgeting. Charter schools, funded with existing per-pupil revenues, have transformed educational programs by hiring head teachers instead of principals, hiring fewer certified teachers and more aides and part-time professionals, using technology to reduce instructional costs, mobilizing community volunteers, and trying a host of other strategies. Alternative schools also have pioneered new and effective approaches to authentically assessing student achievement. Alternative schools repeatedly have proven that they can implement new and effective approaches to student learning and make them work.

Over time, many of these practices have begun to affect traditional public schools. Alternative schools have introduced the concept of educational accountability in public education in a very new and compelling way. They have been instrumental in reducing the often suffocating influence of bureaucratic regulations. Alternative schools pioneered in eliminating the captive audience that results from traditional district boundaries. This has led to the widespread demand for increased choice in public education and, indirectly, to the growing national demand for vouchers, tax credits, and educational competition.

Alternative and magnet schools were the forerunners of the current charter school movement that now has been legislated in more than 20 states. In fact, many of the educators who conceptualized the first charter school legislation and "sold" it to the Minnesota Legislature were national leaders in the alternative school movement.

Much of the pressure for charter schools in various states originated from existing alternative schools, where educators continued to be frustrated by the bureaucratic restraints of state requirements, codes, and administrative rules that often regulate every aspect of public education. In many states, the rules specify the width of the bathroom toilet stalls, the distance between water fountains, the number of minutes teachers must teach specified content areas, the number of hours students must spend in a seat in order to get course credit, the number of days a student can be absent, and on and on. Public schools are smothered with a paralyzing array of restrictions that often force alternative schools to walk a fine line between "exceptional creativity" and bureaucratic compliance in order to maintain their program's integrity.

A growing number of states (Kentucky, Texas, South Dakota, California) have "sunset" existing education policies and have re-established a much different and more general set of principles to govern public education. Many states have passed legislation that authorizes the creation of charter schools in which many state education regulations are replaced with student outcome assessments. There also is a growing movement in some states to bypass reluctant legislators and to place charter school initiatives directly before the voters. John Bierwirth, Superintendent of the Portland, Oregon, Public Schools, has proposed charter status for his entire 57,000-student district. "The district wants the same freedom to propose rules and regulations in the district as the state board of education does for schools in the entire state," he said (Gamble, 1996).

Individual districts in Michigan and entire states, such as Texas, are joining Portland in seeking charter status as the best route to free them from stifling state rules and regulations. While the charter school movement is still relatively new, information and evaluation of these new approaches to public education indicate that as many as 20–25% of charter schools currently in operation are actually converted alternative schools, and that the others have borrowed heavily from the creative approaches to education that were initiated by alternative schools.

The success of alternative public schools has spawned a variety of other educational innovations. And alternative schools continue to serve as a proving ground for innovation, research, and development. As traditional schools continue to seek solutions, alternative schools will provide answers.

MAGNET SCHOOLS AND RESIDENTIAL ALTERNATIVES

During the era of federally mandated school desegregation, alternative schools were identified as the most positive approach, often the only approach, that succeeded in attracting ethnically diverse students and their parents to attend public schools peacefully and effectively. In city after city, under federally mandated desegregation plans, the concept of using high-quality educational programs to attract diverse students and their parents proved to be the only positive effort in the midst of a chaos of bitterness and antagonism. These schools came to be known as magnet schools, and they experienced dramatic growth beginning in the 1970s (Viadero, 1996). Today, school districts across the country continue to use magnet schools to draw diverse students voluntarily into a variety of educational programs in such areas as language immersion, health occupations, technology, aerospace studies, and many others.

A recent national study of student achievement in magnet schools has provided further validation of the concept. Based on comparative data from more than 24,000 eighth- and tenth-grade students in urban high schools, Adam Gamoran (1996) concluded that magnet school students learn more than and out-perform their counterparts in other public schools, as well as those in private and Catholic schools. Gamoran's study is the first to examine cross-district data from public and private schools in major metropolitan areas. Positive school climate, students feeling a sense of membership and belonging, parental support, choice, and a focused curriculum were cited as reasons for the improved performance.

Even more surprising, some communities have found that neighborhoods in the midst of social and economic decline can be revitalized through the introduction of high-quality alternative public schools. Parents are eager to enroll their students in innovative, effective public schools, and many parents have even relocated their families to less affluent neighborhoods so that their children would be close to these popular alternative schools. Many school districts in declining neighborhoods have found that if they establish extended-day schools where parents can drop their children off on their way to work, pick them up at the end of their day, and be assured of having an enriched "before and after school" program, families will relocate to such schools. Alternative schools provide a model that helps unite and strengthen whole communities.

A number of state legislatures, including North Carolina, Louisiana, Alaska, Texas, Maine, and Indiana, have established residential high schools for motivated students in math, science, and international studies. These schools have attracted students from throughout their states. Ball State University in Indiana and the University of North Texas have created state residential alternative schools where students are able to enroll in classes that provide dual credit options and where students can work with leaders in business and industry, as well as with university professors. In Sitka, the Alaska Department of Education operates Mt. Edgecombe School, a residential high school focusing on Pacific Rim studies and serving students from throughout the state. While limited in number, residential alternative schools undoubtedly will experience increasing growth in the future.

UNREALIZED POTENTIAL

> *Trying to operate an alternative school in this community is impossible. They approved our school but really never supported us. They just wanted a place to dump the students that the other schools couldn't deal with. They insist that the rules and regulations that apply to the large schools must apply here. These students need space and individual attention if they're going to succeed, but how do you do that with 22 students in the classroom? And they insist that we enroll more and more of these kids, which really defeats our philosophy of creating a safe environment for our students. I wonder if they really care about these kids at all. It was a great idea originally, but it's not working.*
>
> Alternative High School Teacher,
> Texas

> *We always worried that someone would kick in the door and close us down. Well, it hasn't happened yet; but I feel we're dying a slow death as new regulations and policies make it harder for us to help the students who need it. We now have to turn students away at mid-semester because they have over ten absences at*

their traditional school, a district policy that prohibits them from attending any school. Please explain to me how this helps kids.

Alternative High School Teacher,

Idaho

The potential of alternative schools for revitalizing and restructuring public education has never been fulfilled. With the exception of a few large urban areas with multiple magnet schools, alternative schools continue to be the exception, not the rule. And where charter school legislation has been passed, states have initially limited the number of charter schools that can be started to 50, at most. While almost every school district in the United States has some type of alternative school, only Houston and Los Angeles report that as much as 25% of their entire student body is involved in some type of alternative program. Still, alternative school enrollments are destined to grow. During the years 1995–1996, the states of Missouri, Idaho, and Texas joined several others in enacting legislation intended to expand the presence of alternative schools.

There is also a lamentable dark side to alternative education. Many public school administrators have been unable to resist the temptation to use alternative schools as a subterfuge, perhaps more accurately, to misuse the concept by selectively screening out the more troublesome students from regular classrooms and assigning these difficult children and youth to "special programs." Playing on the alternative "motif," public schools have developed such upbeat names as the "Urban Learning Academy" or the "Alternative Development Center" to describe programs where choice is, in fact, denied and where troublesome youth are selected and assigned. In reality, such programs are not alternative schools. Regardless of what catchy names are used to describe these schools, they often are little more than grim detention centers.

Another problem is that alternative schools have never been widely accepted by teachers, administrators, and local school board members. At the very best, alternative schools operate on the fringe of the local education establishment. They serve comparatively few students and have little effect on mainstream public education. Districts often consider alternative schools as experimental programs that are at the top of the elimination list when there is a budget reduction.

A review of the most recent national directory of alternative public schools indicates that a disappointingly large number of school districts have two or fewer alternative schools. Even in school districts where alternative schools have been established, these programs often serve, at most, 5% of the district's students. While alternative schools work, they are available to only a very small number of American youth.

Even though alternative schools have served as dramatically successful research and development centers, most public school administrators have had great difficulty in "tolerating" alternative schools that stray too far from the norms of mainstream education. Public schools repeatedly have resisted efforts to be changed by approaches that have originated in alternative schools. And in many communities, local school boards have not allowed alternative schools to move beyond established traditions. Often they insist that alternative schools use the established curriculum and grading practices and relate their program to established graduation requirements.

Regrettably, alternative schools sometimes are tacitly perceived as "too" effective. While most public school districts welcome alternatives for at-risk students, many districts become uneasy if those schools begin to attract the "achieving," successful students. In addition, public school educators often are suspicious of programs that succeed for students with whom they have failed.

Alternative schools work. And, as school districts and communities plan and carefully develop new alternatives, they can transform and transcend what public education is all about. Most important, alternative schools can help teach all students effectively, keep more of them in school, help them learn to read, help them feel better about themselves and learning, and help them focus on jobs, careers, and the development of strong, functional families. Alternative schools offer a new vision of hope for public education.

REFERENCES

Barr, R.D. (1981, April). Alternatives for the eighties: A second of development. *Phi Delta Kappan, 62,* 570–573.

Barr, R.D., & Parrett, W.H. (1995). *Hope at last for at-risk youth.* Boston: Allyn & Bacon.

Gamble, C. (1996, March 20). Portland, OR chief calls for all-charter district. *Education Week,* p. 5.

Gamoran, R.A. (1996). Student achievement in public magnet, public comprehensive, and private city high schools. *Educational Evaluation and Policy Analysis, 18* (1), 1–18.

Siebold, K., & Jundson, F. (1996, Summer). The effects of an alternative school on attaining personal success. *Changing Schools.*

Smith, G.R., Gregory, T.B., & Pugh, R.C. (1981, April). Meeting students' needs: Evidence of the superiority of alternative schools. *Phi Delta Kappan, 62,* 561–564.

Viadero, D. (1996, March 6). Students learn more in magnets than in other schools, study finds. *Education Week,* p. 21.

Wehlage, G.G., Rutter, R.A., Smith, G.A., Lesko, N., & Fernandez, R.R. (1989). *Reducing the risk: Schools as communities of support.* Philadelphia: Falmer Press.

West, P. (1996, June 19). Career academies appear to benefit students and teachers. *Education Week*, p. 15.

3

Why Alternative Schools Are So Effective

The student was surly, and it was clear that he did not feel comfortable to be in a school again. He had been expelled from school; and even though he needed only a few credits to graduate, he had not been in school for more than two years.

Student: *I would like to get back to school and get this over with.*

Principal: *That's good. That is exactly what our program is about.*

Student: *Do I have to wait until next January to start?*

Principal: *Why would you want to do that?*

Student: *Every school that I have ever been in started courses only in September and January.*

Principal: *No, at our school you can start any time you like. Do you want to start today?*

Student: *Well, I don't know. I've got a part-time job, and I don't want to be in school all day.*

Principal: *That's fine. You don't have to be in school all day.*

Student: *Really? Every other school that I have ever attended made you be in school all day, and they checked the roll about a thousand times a day to make sure you didn't get away.*

Principal: *Well, here you can come for one course, two courses, or for a full program. You also can work all day on one course; and as soon as you finish it, you get credit for the course.*

Student: *You mean I don't have to wait until June to get credit?*

Principal: *That's exactly right. As soon as you complete a course, you get credit for it.*

Student: *Hey, what time do you open here?*

Principal: *We open at 7:30.*

Student: *How late are you open?*

Principal: *We stay open until 7:30 in the evening.*

Student: *Now let me get this right. If I came in the morning, I could start at 7:30 and work as long as I could until 7:30 in the evening and continue doing that until I finish a course?*

Principal: *That's exactly right.*

Student: *Well, that's great! In a month or so I could complete these courses and then graduate! This is*

incredible! Why don't other schools do this?
understand this. What kind of school is thi
way?

High School Student and Principal,
Vocational Village, Portland, Oregon

THE SEARCH FOR THE IDEAL SCHOOL

ALMOST EVERYONE WANTS TO FIND the ideal school. Everyone wants that particular school where they will fit in and learn best, that matches their needs and is compatible with their interests and goals. Most teachers aspire to teach in a school where there is a shared set of beliefs about how students learn, how to teach effectively, how to discipline and motivate students. Students, too, have a vision about the ideal school—a school where they are respected and safe, where the curriculum relates to their needs, interests, and goals. Parents want that ideal school, and those who can afford it seek out a private or a parochial school that is consistent with their beliefs about how children and youth should be treated and taught.

The problem, of course, is that in the cultural mosaic of the United States, no single school could ever satisfy the beliefs and desires of the many different students, teachers, and families that public education serves. For some students, educators, and parents, the ideal school is an open school; for others it is a traditional school. Some will find that a Montessori school embodies their ideals; for others it is a school with a defined instructional theme or career focus.

There is not and never will be a single, ideal school. However, there are many different ideal schools that respond to the particular needs and interests of different groups of people. Alternative schools permit groups of teachers, students, and parents who share a common philosophy to come together and create their own ideal school. Groups of committed individuals have been doing this for more than 30 years by creating alternative public schools.

CREATING THE IDEAL SCHOOL

Researchers have been unusually successful in identifying exactly how these schools can be created and the essential elements that predict their effectiveness. School districts across the nation have used this information to create effective schools. This rather rare blending of research and practice provides a valid formula by which groups can both create their own personal school and ensure the success of the program. For example, the Hawthorne School (1991), one of the Seattle Public Schools magnet programs, promises parents that if their children maintain attendance and participation, they will be successful. They guarantee it.

The success of alternative schools emanates from a simple proposition: they begin with the needs of the student—each and every student. These schools create a comprehensive support system for students that fosters improved achievement, better attitudes, and regular attendance. The goal of any alternative school is to develop just such a caring community of support, a place where students, teachers, and parents respect one another and are deeply invested in one another's success and the success of the school. Alternative school students, parents, and teachers talk about involvement and ownership. They talk about their school really being "their school." And they speak of exercising choice. Query parents, students, or teachers in an effective alternative school and the response is strikingly consistent: "This is a wonderful school. It reflects who I am. This school is a place where a common vision is shared of what education is all about."

In many ways, alternative schools take on characteristics of a surrogate family. In an age of single-parent households, two working parents, increased mobility, dysfunctional families, growing numbers of children living below poverty levels, and more non-English-speaking children entering school, alternative schools fill a huge void in the lives of youth, both high-risk youth and many who lead more stable lives. Alternative schools provide a place of safety and respect for students, a place to learn and a place to belong. They provide them with an opportunity to create a positive identity.

The classic comparative study, *Reducing the Risk* (1989), which explores the degree to which schools address the human needs of students, showed in the most dramatic manner why alternative schools are so important and effective for their students. In this landmark study of at-risk youth, Gary Wehlage and his associates at the University of Wisconsin suggested that the single most effective educational program was a small alternative school. The reason for this effectiveness was that these types of schools provided students with a "community of support," the very kind of support that the students were lacking in their lives. Wehlage and his colleagues argue that this community of support involves a sense of belonging and a sense of social bonding not only with fellow students and teachers, but also with the school itself. This community of support enables students to become educationally engaged in relevant, meaningful learning in an intimate, small setting.

THE IDEAL SCHOOL AS A "COMMUNITY OF SUPPORT"

Research on alternative schools reports the same type of esprit de corps that is found in elite military organizations, athletic teams, private schools, and even urban youth gangs. Effective alternative schools create an "all for one, one for all" togetherness and support. Alternative school students become committed to their peers and develop a positive environment of subtle pressure to succeed.

Alternative schools accomplish these critical aspects of education by bringing together a group of teachers who are morally committed to educating all students and who choose to become alternative school teachers to gain sufficient autonomy and support to develop programs that respond directly to a wide range of student needs (Wehlage et al., 1989).

It is not unusual to find a high school student "working the phones" in an alternative school early in the morning, checking on her friends to make sure they are awake, out of bed, and preparing for school. Often these "attendance clerks" previously were students in conventional schools who themselves were disruptive and suffering from chronic absenteeism.

A positive school experience will fill a void in a student's life. This function is central to the mission and purpose of alternative public schools. The goal of every effective alternative, magnet, or charter school is to create a caring community of respect and support. When this community of support has been developed, all students have the chance to succeed. They will have found their personal ideal school.

Two decades of collaborative research have served to identify and distill the essential elements necessary to build this community of support. These characteristics enable successful schools to be replicated, expanded, and improved.

A FORMULA FOR SUCCESS

The essential elements of alternative schools have been identified, analyzed, evaluated, and replicated with such success that districts and communities can have total confidence in their investment in an alternative school. If each and every one of the essential elements is carefully considered and implemented, success can be almost guaranteed. Taken together, these essential elements represent a formula for success.

VOLUNTARY PARTICIPATION

I don't think that I'm asking for a lot. No one assigns me and my family to a particular doctor, and I believe that my child's education is just as important as her health. And just as with health issues, I know I need a lot of information about education. I know that I need the advice of my daughter's teachers. I want to know what my options are, the potential of one approach over another. But in the end, I want to be a player. I want to be a part of the decisions about my daughter's education, my daughter's future. I am certainly not an educator any more than I am a medical doctor, but I believe that I would approach decisions about my daughter's school much more carefully and with a good deal more caring than some administrator sitting in an office drawing attendance boundaries for a child he has never met.

Parent,
Seattle, Washington

The greatest power of an alternative school is the simple fact that people choose to participate. No one is assigned; participation is not mandatory. Alternative schools bring democracy to public education; and with democracy comes a welcome, authentic approach to educational accountability. Voluntary participation turns public education inside out: no more captive audiences, no more mandatory school assignments, no more school placements based on where you live, no more selective tracking systems, and no more assigned teachers, curricula, methods of instruction, or schools. The entire system of mandatory teacher and student assignments is replaced by a consumer-driven process based on educational service and sat-isfaction. If one alternative model does not fit the student's needs, the student may find another that does. And while many find this idea very unsettling in the arena of public schooling, it is exactly the system that is used in community colleges, univer-sities, and other forms of higher education. Following high school, students choose their college or university, select a major and often minor course of study, and even select individual teachers. Does this sound revolutionary? Yet public schools rarely have been willing to operate in this manner.

People who can afford private or religious schools have always exercised choice when it comes to their children's educa-tion. So have those who had the time and resources to try home schooling. But unless one resides in a community that has developed public alternative, magnet, or charter schools, most parents, students, and teachers have been denied freedom of choice. Most students have been assigned to a school, a teacher, a curriculum, and an instructional approach regardless of their appropriateness for the child. For the past two centuries, citizens of the United States have had free choice in almost every aspect of their lives with the exception of prisons, the armed forces during a draft, and, unfortunately, the American public schools.

The value of educational choice lies in more than just democracy, political correctness, and educational accountabili-ty. Voluntary participation seems to evoke a powerful commit-ment. Students and teachers who choose to participate in an educational alternative become personally invested in the pro-gram. They become protective of their environment. In the same way that the school serves the parents, students, and teach-ers, the participants bond to serve the school. Voluntary choice encourages teachers and students to try harder to succeed. The school becomes theirs, and they endeavor to make it successful.

EDUCATIONAL DIVERSITY BASED ON STUDENT NEEDS AND INTERESTS

One of our greatest challenges in public education is the growing number of at-risk students, especially teen parents. It's just a monster problem. If a teenager has a child, the odds are she will have a second child in quick succession and be reliant on social services for more than ten years. The likely chance of these babies being uncared for, abused, and educationally disadvantaged is also frightening. So many teen parents are the sons and daughters of teen parents. It's all a tragic, never-ending cycle. But if we can help these young parents stay in school, provide high-quality child care for the infant, teach the young mom basic parenting skills, get them through a GED or high school program and working toward a realistic career, both the kid and their child have a chance to break out of the cycle. To make this happen, schools must be carefully designed to help these girls and their babies. A regular junior high or high school simply will not work. We have to develop programs specifically designed to help these kids.

School Board Member,
Western Oregon

While choice has been identified as an essential component of effective schools, limited choice is not enough. Choice demands diversity. Choice requires commitment. It is essential that districts support a variety of distinctly different educational programs. Furthermore, it is not enough for communities to just allow parents a choice among schools. The programs should be cooperatively designed and developed by the parents, educators, and students who will participate in them.

There also are useful guidelines to aid in the development of diverse educational programs. At the elementary level, alternatives should be developed that address the diverse learning styles, developmental readiness, and progress of children. At the middle through high school levels, alternatives should focus on specific educational needs of students. If students have reading problems, are pregnant, are violent, or have jobs, programs must be developed to address these particular realities of student life. Student needs must define the process of creating the curriculum, the educational goals, and even the organization of the school. Some students and their families may desire a year-round schedule; others may need extended-day programs, evening or Saturday programs, or a program of independent study.

At the high school level, student interest is critical to the design of educational alternatives. Infusing programs with specific career opportunities will generate strong student interest and motivation. Students learn about work, jobs, and careers through apprenticeships, internships, and coursework taught by practitioners. For a student interested in a health profession or a career in media, the arts, engineering, or teaching, to attend a school where the program systematically focuses on these careers bestows invaluable real-world connections to the teaching/learning process. It ensures a far more relevant curriculum and highly motivated teachers and students. It transforms public education from the often dreary learning exercises seemingly unrelated to life outside school into highly focused activities that lead to careers, professions, and productive lives.

CARING AND DEMANDING TEACHERS

*I know all about our students. So many live in poverty,
so many are abused, and they almost all come from
some type of dysfunctional family. But I get so tired of*

people talking about these "poor kids." I think teachers simply use this as an excuse. I can't change their family situation and there is nothing I can do about their parents' income. What I can do is teach their kids. I don't care who they are or where they come from. I love them all and I WILL teach them to read.

Elementary Teacher,
Charleston, South Carolina

One of the most overlooked aspects of the success in alternative schools is that, like students, teachers choose to participate. Alternative schools offer teachers, often for the first time in their careers, the opportunity to select an educational program that reflects their own personal interests and beliefs. To bring together a collection of these "like-minded" teachers expands exponentially the school's potential. Thus an alternative school becomes far more effective as a whole, often overcoming substantial challenges. In fact, most teachers cherish the opportunity to teach in "their ideal school" with colleagues who share their educational philosophy. This undoubtedly is a significant reason why students often perform much better in alternative schools than in their previous public schools.

Regardless of the type of students that an alternative serves—whether they be uninspired to learn in conventional schools, teen parents, high achievers, potential dropouts, or those with a particular career or academic interest—the alternative school allows teachers who care deeply about these students to join together in a small, intimate learning environment. The research is unequivocal on this aspect of alternative schools: If students are surrounded by teachers who both care about them and demand high-quality work, significant learning occurs. Individuals define themselves by the people with whom they interact. To surround students with caring and demanding teachers provides the positive reinforcement and personal motivation that students need to succeed.

In a recent study of expelled students in Colorado, researchers asked the students if they could name one or more teachers during their elementary years who cared about them and worked hard to help them learn. Understandably, even expelled students could recall teachers who cared for them in the self-contained classes of elementary school. Unfortunately, when asked the same question about caring adults at the junior high level, not a single expelled student could identify a caring adult (Colorado Foundation for Families and Children, 1995). This study offers a dramatic insight into the importance of caring adults in the lives of youth. Alternative schools ensure that teachers can care about their students because, like the students, the teachers know why they want to be at that school.

SMALL SCHOOL SIZE

I was just a faceless person in the thousand or so kids in my high school. Nobody knew me, nobody cared. It didn't matter if I came to school or not; no one knew the difference. I didn't really connect with any of the teachers, and I had no friends. I was really just invisible. To leave that place and come to this alternative school was like being welcomed into a warm, caring family. It was like I stopped being the "invisible man" and became a "family man."

10th-Grade Student,
Oregon

There was a time when small schools and low student-teacher ratios dominated public education. Many older people reflect fondly on an era when schools were free from so many of the problems that plague them today. Today, many rural schools and a few urban schools continue to benefit from small enroll-ments and highly personalized classrooms where everyone knows each other and cooperation and respect remain integral components of the learning environment.

Alternative schools, since their conception in the late 1960s, have sought vigorously to maintain small enrollments (usually less than 200 students) and low student-teacher ratios (often 15 or fewer students for each teacher). This environment allows all participants to gain important insights into individual expectations and needs, which in turn fosters a caring, respon-sible atmosphere of educational purpose.

Years of research on school size offer vivid insight into how and why schools affect students. Size of school is a tremen-dously important factor and one that is often overlooked. A key reason that so many students drop out of school or fail academ-ically is that they simply are lost in big, confusing junior/senior high schools. Research has identified "isolates" who always are present in large schools—students who have few friends or who feel that no one cares for or about them. Large schools are per-haps the worst environment for those isolated students. For this reason, the Carnegie Task Force on the Education of Young Adolescents (1989) recommends that large, impersonal junior high schools be divided into a number of small, interdisciplinary groups of teachers and students. The latest report from the National Association of Secondary School Principals, *Breaking Ranks: Changing an American Institution*, recommends that high schools reduce their size to no more than 600 students (Sommerfeld, 1996).

In New York, several urban districts have launched a major effort to transform larger inner-city schools into networks of "mini-schools." Other districts across the nation are joining the Coalition of Essential Schools, which recommends a significantly lower student-teacher ratio and encourages a personalization of learning "to the maximum feasible extent" (Wasley, 1994). School districts across the nation are attempting to make large comprehensive schools smaller, while other districts in Idaho, Alaska, and elsewhere have experienced recent voter rejections of school bonds designed to build more large schools.

Alternative schools with significantly smaller enrollments provide a dramatically different educational environment. Everyone knows one another, and this familiarity tends to foster mutual respect and far less violence. This alone encourages a more personal and humanistic educational program. Whatever else occurs, when starting an alternative school, the originators must ensure that it is organized as a small school.

SHARED VISION

People often think that I'm being very presumptuous when I talk about this as being "my school," but that's exactly how I feel. In my entire life I have never felt that way about any school until now. It is my school. In most schools, parents are simply tolerated; but that's not true here. We spent a year discussing, disagreeing, and developing our vision for the school. But it didn't stop there. We continued to work together to set objectives for our goals, and each semester we evaluated how well we've achieved what we set out to do. I've never been involved in anything like this as a parent in a school. To work with teachers, administrators, students, and other parents to govern the school, build curriculum, evaluate staff, set new policy—it's just an incredible experience. This really is our school!

Parent at an Alternative School,
Portland, Oregon

In recent years, research on improving schools has documented the importance of having parents and teachers develop a shared vision. In conventional public schools, with parental participation defined by the home address, the development of a shared vision may require more than five to seven years of hard work (Levin, 1989). In alternative schools, the development of consensus can occur much faster, because teachers, students, and parents with similar goals and philosophies choose to participate and work in a school together. Parents choose to be there and know what to expect.

Regardless of the time necessary to develop a shared vision for a school, the value of this effort appears well worth the investment. An exciting factor of developing a shared vision for a school is that it often becomes self-fulfilling. When all participants agree on what they expect to achieve and work diligently to monitor progress, they almost always achieve their goals (Barr & Parrett, 1995).

Gardendale Elementary Magnet School in Merritt Island, Florida, spent more than a year creating a vision and strategic plan to guide the improvement of their school. Four years into the completion of the five-year plan, the school staff, parents, and business partners praised the dramatic transformation of their school. Yet they still acknowledged the critical importance of re-evaluation and adjustment in driving their vision toward the school's appointed goals (Narvaez, 1994).

Shared vision provides focus. It allows goals to be established and potential to be reached. Shared vision has long been recognized as a critical factor in business. Alternative schools also accept and value this concept.

SHARED GOVERNANCE/LOCAL AUTONOMY

*It starts with the community. We really could not be
doing this without the support we get from them. But
that support only comes from trust. They trust us to
trust them . . . the community really has a seat at the
table, so to speak. There really isn't anything we decide
for this school that parents, kids, and our community
hasn't been involved in shaping. We trust them . . . and
they trust us.*

Head Teacher at an Alternative High School,
Michigan

There is solid evidence that community participation,
parent involvement, and student commitment will increase
when an authentic atmosphere of school "ownership" is present.
This can occur if school districts transfer authority and autonomy for school governance from the superintendent's office to
the neighborhood school. Providing neighborhood groups of
parents, teachers, and students with the opportunity to participate meaningfully in budgetary, curricular, and instructional
decisions can dramatically increase community, parent, and
student engagement in school. This is even more evident in
alternative and charter schools, where control of curriculum,
instruction, and budget usually is exercised at the school level.
The more authority transferred to the local school, the more
creative the educational approach and the more positive the
educational outcomes.

Local autonomy is essential in developing effective alternative, magnet, and charter school programs. Without local
autonomy and shared governance, schools still are confined by
sometimes paralyzing state and local regulations, such as seat
time. Most important, without local autonomy regarding budget, alternative schools will be prevented from bold innovations.

It is this issue that led to recent demands for charter school legislation. A growing number of parents want a greater role in improving and operating their children's school. An increasing number of communities want "organizations that have sufficient resources and the autonomy to define and act upon a clearly organized agenda for staff and students" (Narvaez, 1994).

CREATIVE INSTRUCTIONAL APPROACHES

High school dropouts leading fourth-graders on environmental field studies along the river? Without teachers? I wouldn't have believed this could work, and certainly wouldn't have enrolled my nine-year-old before seeing it. These high school kids know so much about every aspect of this river and its biology. Obviously, having them teach to classes of elementary students has caused them to become experts! My fourth-grader is now asking me if she'll get to do this in high school.

Elementary School Parent,
Idaho

How instruction is delivered often becomes the deciding factor in a student's participation in the learning process. Central to this concept is the commitment on the part of the alternative school staff to provide a menu of instructional opportunities. The small size of these schools, low pupil-teacher ratios, voluntary enrollment of students, and a focus on addressing individual needs create a framework for delivering a personalized, flexible, and relevant course of study—a course of study that offers many students their first opportunity to connect with educators in a serious learning partnership. The following approaches characterize instructional delivery in effective alternative schools.

Focus on individual needs. All students possess a complex array of needs and academic abilities. Alternative schools begin the learning partnership through a careful assessment of these needs and abilities and prescribe an initial schedule of goals and participation that connects the student with the instructional opportunities of the school.

Opportunities to accelerate learning/catch up. Through the development of a range of formal and informal opportunities, the students can structure a program of study that allows them to learn as fast as they can. A few of these opportunities include intensive tutoring in reading to reach grade level; an internship with an accountant to apply advanced mathematical skills and investigate a career; an interdisciplinary course in U.S. literature and government that meets two graduation requirements; the opportunity to study independently six to ten hours a day to catch up in physical science; and the chance to focus complete attention on preparing for a GED, ACT, or SAT.

Creative use of time. For many alternative schools, the doors open at 7 a.m. and close at 10:30 p.m. Throughout the day, students are provided with a learning environment that accommodates work, child care, transportation, and sleeping schedules. Credit is earned by academic achievement, rather than seat time, as students take increased responsibility for meeting their educational goals. Flexible use of time and schedules also provides for individual staff/student contact, as well as staff planning and professional development. The school sets the "clock" based on student needs and the realities of their lives.

Diverse instructional practices. While every alternative school is unique, a commitment to choice, active learning, and diversity in instructional practice characterizes all programs. Again, from a needs-based perspective, the practices range from traditional forms of direct instruction to independent learning.

Individual and group projects, small cooperative groups, student learning contracts, internships, apprenticeships, and an array of tutoring arrangements represent several of the more common practices of alternative schools.

Involving students as resources. Alternative schools have had great success in involving students in powerful new ways. Alternative schools involve students as peer tutors and tutors for younger children. They involve students in real-life practice in senior citizen centers, hospitals, government offices, etc. They involve students in serving as small-business entrepreneurs, creating and operating their own business enterprises. They allow students to participate in significant ways in school governance and curriculum development. Alternative schools often encourage students to plan and teach special-interest courses at their school.

One of the well-known stories about alternative schools involves the elementary students at the St. Paul Open School—they planned, designed, raised money for, and built their own school playground. The older students at the St. Paul Open School also operated a "Consumer Protection Program." The students operated a hotline and received calls from consumers throughout the metropolitan area who felt they had been deceived or defrauded. The students then conducted intensive background investigations to try to identify the problems and solve them.

Alternative school programs should plan ways to involve students in adult and real-world responsibilities. Research on this type of experience has documented long-term, positive effects for students.

It has been clearly documented that creative instructional approaches that match the needs of each student improve the achievement and educational success of the increasingly diverse student population of America's schools. The degree to which an alternative school can deliver instructional choices has a direct relationship to the academic success of its clientele.

RELEVANT/FOCUSED CURRICULUM

All I'm saying is that I know what I want to do some-day. I want to be an engineer. I'm great in math and wish that I could take some courses that relate to engi-neering. Wood shop is all right. It's kind of fun. But I guarantee you that I'm never going to be a carpenter when I grow up. I may be only a kid, but I can figure that out. Come on, give me a break. Let me study something that's relevant.

Middle School Student,
Fort Worth, Texas

Implementing a relevant and focused curriculum and continually improving it is critical to the success of an alternative school. One of the primary reasons middle and high school students drop out, and perhaps the most frequent complaint of those who remain, is that school is boring, that it has little to do with the "real" world. Alternative schools succeed by meaningfully connecting students with an active, relevant curriculum. These curricula are focused on individual needs, basic skill acquisition, academic preparation linked to careers, and authentic opportunities for students to participate in the design and delivery of the learning environment.

While every curriculum varies, essential components of effective curricula include some degree of emphasis in each of the following areas.

Basic skills through advanced academic preparation. Alternative schools, like their traditional counterparts, serve a diverse range of student academic levels. Key to a program's success is the initial assessment of needs and the provision of an individualized program to accelerate a student's acquisition of basic skills. While the skills involved in literature and mathematics often receive substantial attention initially, the students also benefit from a focus on high-interest studies. Thus opportunities for advanced academic study and experience become much more acceptable to the school and relevant to the student.

Interdisciplinary, thematic content. For decades, alternative schools have offered an interdisciplinary, thematic approach to content. Few areas of life can be pigeonholed within the confines of an academic discipline; the content of curricula in alternative schools reflects that reality. What is most important is that the students develop the critical thinking skills necessary to apply knowledge to the complex circumstances of real life. Thus alternative schools, while acknowledging the expectations of the approved district curriculum, actively seek means of creating new curricula that extend district requirements to address the multiple intelligences and needs of the students.

Out-of-school learning. Such pioneer alternative school programs as the Philadelphia Parkway School, the Chicago Metro School, and other schools without walls demonstrated the power and relevance of learning in real-life settings. In these early alternatives, students rarely went to classes in schools. Their classrooms were located throughout the city in banks, museums, hospitals, government offices, and boardrooms. Public school teachers were supplemented by bankers, curators, doctors, politicians, and business leaders. This tradition has become even more sophisticated and effective in urban magnet schools that are located in hospitals, television stations, or local theaters. The Foxfire Program in Rabun Gap, Georgia, enables rural students to become amateur anthropologists, collecting local history and folklore. Recently, alternative schools have been using the Internet as their community to collect, record, and report environmental and weather data as part of world-wide student research projects.

To enrich student learning and increase motivation, out-of-school learning experiences should be an important part of any alternative school. Many alternative schools include student participation in community service as a graduation requirement. For years, students in alternative schools have learned invaluable lessons about citizenship, community participation, and life through projects designed to improve their community and its environment. Examples include internships in nursing homes, hospitals, and Head Start programs; group projects concerning the environment; Habitat for Humanity projects; and apprenticeships and field experiences throughout the helping professions. Business projects also serve as exceptional opportunities to connect all areas of the curriculum to the real world. These range from the typical student operation of a school store or concession to a complete international business in smoked salmon export and silk import.

Understanding and using technology. Not only have technological advances dramatically changed the workplace and daily lives of our nation, but they have virtually mandated that schools be restructured. The personal computer has become essential to life and work in developed countries. Failing to teach the skills needed to use this technology would be commensurate with schools of the past ignoring the availability of the printed word. Alternative schools, ranging from dropout-prevention programs through advanced technological magnets, must be committed to incorporating these tools throughout the curriculum.

An emphasis on healthy lives. Many alternative schools have long embraced a comprehensive approach to integrating programs and content that promote healthful living through informed decision making. While the concept of "full-service schools" is only recently receiving serious consideration in America's traditional schools, alternative programs for decades have sought to incorporate awareness, service, and intervention programs into the school curriculum. Such topics as alcohol and drugs, sexually transmitted disease, suicide prevention, conflict resolution, parenting, pre- and postnatal care, nutrition, gangs and violence, racism and hate behaviors, and others are addressed through counseling, peer groups, organized programs, and out-of-school learning projects. Effective alternative schools educate the "whole" student and thus do not exclude the realities of life from school.

Transition to work. Alternative schools, especially urban magnet programs, have become the model in helping students make the transition from public school to the world of work. Alternative schools are pioneers in integrating high school education with a highly focused program of career development. Recent research on career-oriented magnet schools has demonstrated what a powerful motivation this type of integration can be. When high school students can combine their high school education with a personal interest in a particular career, they become highly motivated, find their education to be very relevant, and increase their academic achievement. Academic achievement in career-focused magnet schools is far higher than it is in other types of high schools, both public and private.

COMPREHENSIVE PROGRAMS

If we didn't have a day care program for our teen parents, they wouldn't be here. And if they weren't here, they wouldn't be in school in this district. These students have so many needs that come before algebra. We counsel, advise, refer for medical needs, help with taxes, tutor, assist with work orientation and placements . . . .

We couldn't do this if the staff weren't committed to helping these students with all that stuff that often inhibits any desire to do academic work. We can teach algebra because we deal with the other stuff.

Teacher, Teen Parent Program,
New Mexico

Alternative schools should be available throughout the K–12 school years. They are especially important for at-risk children. Unfortunately, one of the most common mistakes when starting an alternative school is to try to "fix kids up" in a short time and get them back into the regular program. School administrators and school boards often refer to alternative schools as "transition programs," that is, the goal is to take troublemakers or students with learning problems out of the traditional program, "repair them," and then place the students back into the traditional schools. While returning to regular classes always should be an option for students—and some will choose to return—most at-risk students have taken years to arrive at their current conditions, and there is no quick fix for their problems.

Without alternative schools, many students manage to succeed marginally through the elementary years, only to be lost in large, impersonal junior high schools. Most districts have few choices at the elementary and junior high levels; thus students must endure a decade of difficulty before they have an opportunity to attend an alternative school. By that time, their problems often are dramatic. The middle-level years may well be the most important time for students to have an opportunity to attend an alternative school. Yet few school districts offer alternative programming at that level.

Effective schools have developed coordinated programs with appropriate social service agencies in order to become "full-service schools." These schools typically provide health services for students and often use the "case management" approach to identify student/family needs and to seek help and support from a wide range of community agencies.

Many alternative schools have created "youth councils" that include representatives from a variety of social service agencies. These youth councils meet weekly or monthly to review the problems and needs of individual students and their families. Council actions can lead to health services, eyeglasses, inoculations, food stamps, clothing, and even temporary housing for homeless families.

Alternative schools are not just a stopgap for temporary problems. They are most effective when they are available throughout the K–12 program.

STUDENT ASSESSMENT

> *Let me tell you, it is so funny to work with legislators regarding charter schools. After you talk with them awhile, you can see "light bulbs" coming on over their heads. They will interrupt and ask some really basic question, like, "Do you mean to tell us that you are proposing to actually assess student learning rather than count up course credits?" Suddenly they will just snap into focus. It's like the old children's story, "The Emperor's New Clothes." Legislators suddenly recognize that "the dude is nude," that the traditional approach to student assessment in public education is totally bankrupt.*

> Charter School Lobbyist,
> California

For decades, alternative, magnet, and charter schools have sought to authentically assess student achievement. Nongraded classrooms, portfolios, projects, graduation competencies, walka-bouts, community service, and narrative appraisals are examples of the methods developed by alternative school educators to assess student achievement. Rather than assessing learning on the basis of "seat time" in courses, on credits earned, or by student grades, alternative, magnet, and charter schools have pioneered new approaches to assessing progress toward graduation.

So important is this effort that more than 20 state legis-latures have been willing to waive the usual regulations that gov-ern public education if districts replace them with improved means of assessing student learning. Governors, state legislators, and university officials in these states have concluded that few of the usual regulations that govern public education really matter if students can graduate from public schools illiterate and unemployable.

Rather than looking at student transcripts, some schools now assess precisely what the students have learned. For charter schools, their financial contract with the state or a school district actually depends on the documentation of student learning and achievement. The school is penalized and will face revocation of its charter if the students do not learn. While most educators express a desire to teach all students, not only are charter schools expected to do so, but their contract requires them to do it.

Some of America's alternative schools pioneered this idea. During the late 1960s, one of the nation's first alternative schools, the St. Paul Open School, replaced high school gradua-tion requirements with a set of a dozen graduation competen-cies. Rather than earning credit by spending a year in a course with a passing grade, the Open School developed a process by which students, teachers, and parents developed individualized plans for students to pursue each of the graduation competen-cies. Each year, students met with school officials to determine whether satisfactory progress was being made toward the competencies, and plans would be made to continue their work until they had satisfactorily achieved the competencies. Almost 30 years later, this approach is still in place, though the competencies have now been expanded to a total of 18 and the process has been refined so that students demonstrate through a critical review that they have achieved necessary competencies. The school's required competencies are listed on page 54.

Recently, some states have established statewide assessment exams or standards at selected grade levels. These evaluations are sometimes referred to as "barrier tests." Such statewide testing enables policymakers to compare student learning among different schools and districts. The state of Kentucky has explored incentive payments to teachers and schools who achieve unusually high student gains. Merit pay, step increases on salary tables, and career ladder opportunities represent ways to reward educators who demonstrate achievement with their classes and students. But this approach usually suffers from the basic problems associated with the use of standardized tests, such as incongruity of content with local curriculum, the environment, culture, teacher biases, and student and parent indifference. However, statewide testing does enable comparisons of alternative schools not only with other public schools but also with private and parochial schools. Thus it undoubtedly will maintain a prominent influence in education policy.

Despite this widespread use of standardized assessments, alternative schools continue to develop and use innovative practices to monitor student learning. They do this partly to ensure that every student achieves to his or her capacity, but also to evaluate the effectiveness of the diverse instructional approaches and curricula employed in these schools.

ST. PAUL OPEN SCHOOL GRADUATION PROCESS: SUMMARY OF VALIDATIONS

Post High School Plans

Employment-Seeking Skills

Information Finding

Career Investigation

Service to the School

Group Process

Healthy Body

Coherent Communication

Mathematics

Science and Technology

Learning from the Community

Service to the Community

Current Issues

Consumer Awareness

Cultural Awareness (Student's)

Cultural Awareness (Selected Minority)

Cultural Awareness (Student's Choice)

High School Summary

—St. Paul Open School
1993 Program Guidelines

Alternative, magnet, and charter schools represent the frontier of authentic educational assessment, where measuring what a student learns is never delegated solely to a standardized test. Student assessment is embraced as a vital partner in teaching all students.

GUARANTEEING SUCCESS THROUGH ALTERNATIVE SCHOOLS

Research has been so effective in identifying the essential components of effective alternative schools that it is now possible to all but guarantee program effectiveness. Alternative schools work, and we know why they work. The unique interaction of choice, small size, caring and demanding teachers, and other identified elements are essential building blocks of a powerful, effective school. It is this type of school that creates the support system that all American youth deserve.

REFERENCES

Barr, R.D., & Parrett, W.H. (1995). *Hope at last for at-risk youth.* Boston: Allyn & Bacon.

Carnegie Task Force on the Education of Young Adolescents. (1989). *Turning points: Preparing youth for the 21st Century.* Waldorf, MD: Carnegie Council on Adolescent Development.

Colorado Foundation for Families and Children. (1995). *School expulsions: A cross-systems problem.* Denver: Author.

Hawthorne School. (1991). Unpublished evaluation report. Seattle: Author.

Levin, H.M. (1989). *Accelerated schools: A new strategy for at-risk students* (Policy Bulletin No. 6). Bloomington, IN: Consortium on Educational Policy Studies.

Narvaez, A., Jr. (1994). A gem of choice. *Educational Leadership, 52* (1), 9–11.

Sommerfeld, M. (1996, February 28). Report calls for personal touch in high school. *Education Week*, p. 9.

Wasley, P.A. (1994). *Stirring the chalkdust.* New York: Teachers College Press.

Wehlage, G.G., Rutter, R.A., Smith, G.A., Lesko, N., & Fernandez, R.R. (1989). *Reducing the risk: Schools as communities of support.* Philadelphia: Falmer Press.

4

Established Alternative School Models

The best education money can't buy.

Motto of the Houston Public Schools
Magnet Programs

ALTERNATIVE SCHOOLS come in all sizes and shapes. There is literally something for everyone. Some alternatives focus on different instructional approaches; others address the needs of specific types of students, a particular curriculum or career focus, unusual learning opportunities in a particular community, or some form of service to the community. There are alternatives that focus on a particular grade level, different calendars, the daily schedules, and multiple means to organize and administrate the alternative program. Many alternatives involve an eclectic collection of different aspects of many types of schools to form their unique character. While many programs are similar, virtually no two schools are identical.

School districts have developed this vast array of alternatives in order to ensure that all students have an opportunity to attend the school of their choice, work successfully to their potential, and graduate. Because the needs and interests of students vary significantly, school districts have found it necessary to provide a broad range of educational programs and to make these learning opportunities available throughout the day, evening, and year round. Public education in many communities has, by necessity, become a 7:00 a.m. to 10:30 p.m. enterprise. Recognizing that this type of "service" approach to public education is a birthright of American youth, many states now require school districts to offer a range of alternative programs and often provide financial incentives to develop and operate these alternatives. A number of states require school districts to develop alternative programs for suspended, expelled, or incarcerated youth; and more than 20 states have passed charter school legislation that permits the development of public schools that may be virtually free from burdensome state rules and regulations.

It is important to remember that when a district has a large number of alternatives, its conventional schools likewise become distinct options. Parents and students have the ability to choose to attend the conventional schools just as they choose the alternatives.

The most important issue in starting an alternative, magnet, or charter school is identifying or developing an appropriate theme or educational model—a model that will attract the necessary numbers of students, parents, and educators to create a viable program. The model must be sufficiently defined to provide the necessary consensus of support. The better the school is defined, the clearer the type of program that is being proposed or developed and the easier it is to communicate the concept to students, parents, teachers, school board members, school administrators, and the community.

Name recognition is often critical in establishing a new program and attracting support. For this reason, there is great value in considering well-defined models that have a strong track record of success. There is also the added value for any new school to network with other similar programs. Some types of alternatives have national organizations to provide resources, support, and staff development. These established alternatives usually have books, articles, research and evaluation reports, newsletters, and annual conferences that can provide direct support for a new school.

Several alternative models are so well-known that most school districts will have many parents and teachers who are familiar with them, such as Montessori schools, dropout prevention programs, performing arts academies, year-round schools, and traditional fundamental programs. In these cases, a single announcement that such a school is being developed can create an immediate show of support. In addition, groups of well-informed parents may approach a school board or superintendent and request the development of a particular alternative that is available in a neighboring community or in a community where they previously lived.

Replicating an established alternative model is often far more feasible when skeptical school board members or school administrators can visit and observe successful programs. What so often seems to traditional educators to be an unusual, revolutionary, or perhaps even irresponsible concept for a school often can be transformed into a reasonable, appropriate concept simply by visiting a successful model in another school district.

For parents, students, and educators attempting to choose a school, as well as for districts and communities that are exploring possibilities in order to start or expand educational choices, a review of the many types of successful alternative, magnet, and charter schools is the appropriate place to begin. For these reasons, a sample of some of the most established alternative models has been organized. This collection, while far from all-inclusive, should help school and community representatives explore the range of well-established alternatives that exist for possible use.

ALTERNATIVES THAT FOCUS ON INSTRUCTIONAL APPROACHES

While alternatives that focus on different instructional approaches can be found at all levels, including K–12 alternatives, they most often characterize alternatives at the elementary level. It is at the early ages that different learning and teaching styles can be so important. However, junior and senior high schools also are developing programs based on instructional styles.

Each of the following instructional approaches reflects a different philosophy of teaching and learning and is supported by conclusive research. Each approach has been tested and has a track record of positive evaluation. Some of these instructional approaches seem to work best with certain types of children, and learning appears to be maximized when teaching styles and learning styles are matched. Alternatives that focus on instructional approaches include:

Montessori Schools: Based on the ideas of Italian physician/educator Maria Montessori, these schools have become highly sophisticated and successful (Montessori, 1967). Not only do Montessori schools share a particular set of beliefs about child growth and development and a highly structured approach to learning based on human development, these schools also follow an established curriculum and use carefully developed instructional materials, manipulatives, toys, and games. Montessori schools require teachers to be trained and certified in the Montessori approach. Three national associations, the American Montessori Society, Association Montessori International, and the North American Montessori Teacher's Association, support more than 5,000 private Montessori schools by providing teacher preparation, credentialing, and professional development opportunities.

While Montessori schools usually are private schools, the success of this method, coupled with a growing educational sophistication of parents, has led to an increased consumer demand for public Montessori schools. The first Montessori public schools were established in Cincinnati and Indianapolis in the early 1970s, and today more than 200 operate throughout the United States. In 1988, Cleveland State University and the North American Montessori Teacher's Association, an organization of more than 2,200 private and 175 public Montessori schools, developed the Montessori Public School Consortium, a clearinghouse for implementing the Montessori method in public schools. The consortium is a part of the North American Montessori Teacher's Association and can be contacted at 11424 Bellflower Road NE, Cleveland, OH 44106; or call (216) 421-1905 (Kahn, 1993).

Open Schools: Open schools in the United States grew out of interest in similar programs in Great Britain, particularly the British Infant School. Based in part on the ideas of educators John Holt, Roland Barth, and Charles Rathbone, today's open schools work to counter traditional education, which they believe is often too impersonal and external to the child. Open educators believe that, since education is a natural experience, learning comes from within. At best, teachers are believed to be facilitators of naturalistic, developmental learning (Rathbone, 1971).

Open schools in the United States tend to be developed around classroom learning centers. Young children are encouraged to pursue their own curiosity and inquisitiveness, select learning activities, and to some extent, decide where and how long they will pursue those activities.

The St. Paul Open School (1971) was one of the first public school alternatives in the United States. Based on the landmark education research effort of the 1940s, the Eight Year Study, the St. Paul Open School created a model that has served as the benchmark for developing open schools throughout North America. Wayne Jennings and Joe Nathan, the school's first principal and curriculum director, continue to be recognized as pioneers in the alternative public school movement. Their latest efforts have included leading the conceptual development and political approval of the nation's first charter school legislation in Minnesota (1991) and working with a network of boundary-breaking schools, Designs for Learning. The St. Paul Open School, a K–12 program, was one of the first in the nation to successfully replace graduation requirements with a set of required graduation competencies.

Other nationally recognized alternative open schools are the Metropolitan Learning Center, a K–12 liberal arts open school in Portland, Oregon, and the K–12 Brown School in Louisville, Kentucky.

Continuous Progress Schools: Research during the past 15 years has helped educators to understand the unfortunate effects of retaining or "holding back" young children who have not mastered basic skills. Given an increasing understanding of human growth and development and a growing body of brain research, educators have attempted to rethink and restructure the early grade levels to accommodate the various developmental levels of young children. While almost all parents and educators recognize that young children learn to walk and talk at very different ages, schools have traditionally ignored the great developmental differences in young children and expect them all to learn to read at precisely the same time. Rather than retaining children who have not mastered the essential curriculum, schools have experimented with a variety of nongraded, multi-aged groupings of children, usually during the first four years of school.

Multi-aged groupings take the pressure off ensuring that all children learn the basics on a calendar schedule and enable schools to highly individualize teaching and learning. Each student is able to pursue learning at his or her own rate, and most children will progress at very different rates across the various subject areas. A second-grader may be doing third- or fourth-grade math but still be struggling with reading. Each child is encouraged to progress as far and as fast as possible.

The programs typically set a goal to ensure that all children have learned to read at grade level and have mastered appropriate basics by the end of the third or fourth grade. Some schools randomly group students in grades 1–3 or 1–4; other schools use multi-age grouping arrangements to join various combinations of two to three grade levels.

One of the first efforts to create a nongraded public school was started in southeast Minneapolis during the late 1960s. Today, state legislation in Oregon and Kentucky has called for comprehensive use of nongraded, continuous progress elementary schools. As of spring 1996, 67% of Oregon's elementary schools offer some form of nongraded instruction, doubling the number reported in 1993. Most districts throughout the country now offer some form of multi-age instruction at the elementary level. This concept also is dominant throughout the spectrum of alternative elementary, middle, and K–12 schools.

Traditional/Fundamental Schools: Because some young children seem to need more structure and drill, school districts throughout the United States began to model private and parochial schools by developing schools that emphasize fundamental, basic education. These schools often have strict dress codes or require uniforms. In addition, they often have strict homework requirements, expectations for parents, and behavior expectations. Where these schools are available, parents who are frustrated by what they consider to be lax discipline and the "fun and games" approach to public education have been eager to enroll their children in schools characterized by discipline, rigorous attention to the basics, and high expectations. Traditional/fundamental schools are supported by the National Council for Basic Education.

For many years, traditional/fundamental schools were started in Louisville, Kentucky, at the elementary level. Later, the Jefferson County School District in Louisville developed traditional middle and high schools. Today, the most requested alternative schools in the Jefferson County School District continue to be traditional schools. The Barret Traditional Middle School in Louisville gained national recognition for providing every child with a laptop computer and requiring that students become computer literate. The Louisville Male Traditional High School continues to be highly regarded by parents and students as the district's premier traditional high school.

Self-Directed Learning: In many communities, there is a small but determined group of parents and students who believe strongly in self-initiated, self-directed study. Thirty years ago, these individuals helped to create what came to be known as the "free school movement" in the United States. While most of the free schools were established as private schools, a number of communities developed public school alternatives where learning was not imposed "on" but created "with" students. During the 1960s, these schools often reflected the "counter-culture" of the times and emphasized student freedom to choose what and how they learned. These schools often emphasized free expression in art, music, and writing.

The philosophy of free schools was based initially on the writing of A.S. Neill. In his widely read book, *Summerhill* (1977), Neill described his work in a British private school where students were free to learn or not to learn. Paralleling Neill's work, American educators James Herndon, Herb Kohl, John Holt, and other compassionate critics attacked the inhumane and destructive influence of what they considered the irrelevant teaching and educational practices of conventional schools. As a group, they labored for a better way to teach our children.

In recent years, this concept has emerged in a number of different forms. Many home schoolers, wary of the effects of public education, support the concept of self-directed learning in the privacy of their homes. More typically, this philosophy is found in programs that use individualized learning contracts, correspondence, and independent study. Many times, students who prefer this approach are very independent and self-motivated. Others are attracted to the approach because their jobs make it difficult, or impossible, to attend school during the scheduled class times. The growing sophistication of computer technology and increasing accessibility to the Internet have greatly expanded opportunities for this option.

There are public schools that emphasize the learning freedom philosophy. In Vancouver, Washington, the local district has created "the Eagle Wing," an alternative school within a school. In this unusual school, rather than attend classes, students develop learning goals and conduct independent study and personal and small-group investigations. At Pan Terra Alternative in Vancouver, a dropout prevention school, students develop learning contracts and pursue learning goals that may include classroom learning and independent study, as well as related practical experiences. For many years, the Seattle Public Schools have operated an alternative called the Off-Campus School, where students pursue independent learning in the required subject areas and periodically schedule time with teachers to discuss their learning and assess their progress. Numerous districts, particularly those in remote rural areas, for years have employed correspondence study and itinerant teachers as a necessary means of providing education.

Students who make the transition to nondirected or independent learning often experience difficulty for the first few months. With the exception of young children, almost all school-age students become thoroughly conditioned to "passive learning," that is, someone else plans lessons, selects material, and tries to motivate students to learn. Even students who feel bored and frustrated by traditional teacher-dominated classrooms may find it extremely difficult to make the transition to self-directed learning. Most students take several months to become accustomed to the lack of direction; and during this time the teacher, the student, and parents often experience anxiety due to uncertainty over the student's learning. Trying to translate the individualized, and often interdisciplinary, independent study of students into traditional course requirements for graduation also poses a problem. Despite these challenges, self-directed learning provides a viable option for many parents and students.

Waldorf Schools: An international alternative education movement was inspired by the ideas of German educator Rudolph Steiner. More than a hundred such schools operate today in North America, though all are private schools. Steiner's ideas focused on what he called "spiritual science," which explored the archetypal and transpersonal dimensions of reality. His ideas have been used in medicine, architecture, agriculture, and education.

A Waldorf School (named after a grant by the owner of the Waldorf Astoria Company) uses a highly structured program that focuses on the child's intellectual, emotional, and spiritual needs. A teacher often will begin working with students at the first-grade level and stay with them for eight years. Waldorf Schools use art, storytelling, mythology, and many movement activities in their educational program. Children are encouraged to engage the world through imagination and physical activity, rather than through abstract intellectual concepts.

While Waldorf Schools in the United States are exclusively private, the concepts could be developed into an alternative public school. There are currently 97 full member and affiliated Waldorf Schools in the United States and Canada and an additional 45 schools for young children and kindergartners. There are also four Waldorf teacher education centers in the United States (Association of Waldorf Schools of North America, n.d.).

Paideia Schools: In 1982 the renowned philosopher Mortimer Adler outlined a rigorous approach to public education. The proposal emphasized a single-track, liberal arts educational program designed to prepare students for work, citizenship, and lifelong learning. The school prepares all students for further postsecondary education. Paideia education is based on three "columns" of learning—didactic teaching, socratic questioning, and coaching (Adler, 1982). The goal is for 80% of learning to be student-centered.

In 1984 the Chattanooga, Tennessee, School District established a magnet program based on the Paideia concept. The district established the School for the Arts at the middle school level, then in 1988 added a 10th-grade and later a K–4 program. In 1991 the school district created a second Paideia school, a K–8 School for the Liberal Arts, and later established Paideia Schools as neighborhood schools (Phoenix Paideia Schools) and as a fine arts and performing arts magnet school.

Multiple Intelligences Schools: In numerous books over a period of eight years, Harvard psychologist Howard Gardner developed and refined the concept of multiple intelligences. Concerned that most schools did not truly educate students, Gardner proposed an educational approach based on seven areas of intellectual development: linguistics, musical, logical/mathematical, spatial, bodily/kinesthetic, interpersonal, and intrapersonal (Gardner, 1983, 1989, 1991).

In 1984, eight teachers in Indianapolis worked together to create a public school based on the ideas of Gardner. This elementary program, called the Key School, received considerable national attention, including an article in the National Education Association (NEA) journal that suggested that the Key School might be the best school in the country. The Key School emphasizes the development of multiple intelligences. It is theme-based, uses an integrated curriculum, has nongraded classrooms, uses a project approach, and employs portfolio-based assessment. The school focuses on enrichment instead of remediation, encourages motivation, uses technology extensively, requires a second language for middle school students, has a fully integrated arts program, makes extensive use of community resources, and uses a qualitative approach to evaluate students. A second school focusing on multiple intelligences, the Renaissance Middle School, recently has been created as an outgrowth of the original Key School. Due to popular demand, the Indianapolis-based Key schools provide summer workshops for other educators interested in starting similar schools.

Howard Gardner is working with the Coalition of Essential Schools and other school reform groups to develop other types of schools that emphasize multiple intelligences, currently referred to as ATLAS schools.

ALTERNATIVES THAT FOCUS ON THE NEEDS AND INTERESTS OF STUDENTS

> *The blonde girl in the back desk is smarter than me. The boy by the window is always angry. The messy-haired girl has sex with her father. That child is loved by both parents. This one forgot his medication, while that one "self-medicates." The sleepy-looking one watches TV all night. The young-looking girl is a perfectionist. The parents of the one looking out the window are getting a divorce. That one's father died last year. The smiling one can't learn enough and that one can't read. What can I teach these children?*
>
> Teacher at North Junior High,
> Boise, Idaho

The vast majority of alternative schools in the United States are designed to address the unique needs of a particular type of student. While many of these schools also involve career themes, their primary distinction grows out of an effort to meet the needs of the students they serve. Some schools serve teen parents and pregnant students; others serve students who are far behind academically, who have already dropped out of school, or who are incarcerated. Some schools address the needs of highly motivated and talented students; others are designed for students highly skilled in the arts. These schools provide school programs and services that ensure the success of all students. If students have drug or alcohol problems, the schools provide extensive substance-abuse education programs, support groups, and counseling services and often are affiliated with a treatment center. If students are pregnant or are parents, the instructional program will focus on pre- and postnatal care, nutrition, and health and often will provide infant and child care to enable parents to attend academic classes. If students are motivated and talented in math and science, they may attend residential high schools and work directly with professional engineers and scientists.

Teen Parent Schools:

"Listen," she said, "these teen moms couldn't care less about school." Then holding her hand up, the director of the Teen Parent Program ticked off items one by one on each finger. "Most of these young women don't have a job, don't have child care, and most don't have a phone or a car or, perhaps worse, they have a car that doesn't work. They are all on food stamps or welfare, or both; many have been kicked out of their homes and have no place to live, many of them are sick, their babies are sick, and they have no health care. And most have been abused by their father, their boyfriend, or sometimes by both; and they all have this screaming, demanding little hellion with a dirty diaper on. You think they are interested in continuing their education? Get real! Dealing with teen parents is a monster problem. If we have any hope of helping these kids and their babies, we have to do the wildest things. We have

to find a safe place for them to live, seek out all types of social services for them, go pick them up and take them home and provide health care and be very, very careful that we don't schedule anything during the afternoon soap operas or Oprah. That, my friend, is the heart and guts of a first-rate teen parent program. In this world, you get real, real quick or you get out of the business."

Director, Teen Parent Program,
Salem, Oregon

Serving the needs of teenage parents or pregnant teenagers may well be the most demanding job in public education. Not only do the students face the usual challenges of learning, earning credit, and graduating, they now have or soon will have an infant or young child to care for. Often these students are poor; they usually do not have adequate health services available. They usually have no child care, and many may not even have a home. Without carefully designed schools to address the many needs of the teen parent or pregnant teenager, these students almost always will drop out of school, have more children, and be on some form of public assistance for years, sometimes decades. And all too often, their children also grow up in poor and often dysfunctional settings only to perpetuate the cycle of despair into the next generation.

Perhaps the most widely recognized and thoroughly studied teen parent program in the United States is the New Futures School in Albuquerque, New Mexico. Opening its doors in 1970, this school continues to be a model of community organization. Over the past 23 years, New Futures has helped more than 4,000 adolescents to progress through the difficult experience of teen pregnancy and parenthood. The school features an academic program that leads to a regular diploma or a

GED course for older students, an in-school clinic that provides for mothers' health and parental needs, counseling services, a child care facility, and a career exploration/jobs program. The National School Boards Association highlighted the success of this program.

> *A five-year follow-up study conducted in 1987 of students who attended the school showed that 73 percent had graduated from high school (an additional 4 percent were still in school) and more than half (54 percent) went on to postsecondary education programs. Ninety-seven percent of New Futures students in 1980–87 passed the state-mandated high school proficiency exam. Students' health and child-rearing practices also improved: they had comparatively fewer repeat pregnancies and fewer low-birth-weight babies, and more than half breastfed their babies.* (National School Boards Association, 1989, p. 36).

Dropout and Dropout Prevention Alternatives: The oldest form of alternative school focused on the school dropout and the potential dropout. These early schools often were referred to as continuation schools and eagerly recruited students from the jailhouse steps, juvenile courts, and street corners. Today, dropout and dropout prevention programs represent the largest number of alternative public schools in the United States. Almost every school district, regardless of how small or how isolated, will have some type of dropout prevention program or have access to one. Many states require school districts to have such programs, which also may serve habitual troublemakers and expelled students.

These schools often have a tremendous positive effect on students who have not done well in traditional academic settings. Some of the greatest success stories come from these alternative programs and schools. For students who have never been academically successful, participation in a high-quality alternative school typically will lead to impressive, often astounding academic gains. Many such schools use tutoring, high-interest curricular material, self-paced learning, and high school equivalency exams to enable students who are far behind academically to catch up, accelerate their learning, and graduate from high school. Some of these schools use behavior modification to enable students to gain tangible rewards for positive, constructive behavior and academic success. These schools often operate from early morning to late evening, provide for individual contract learning, maintain small classes, and provide health services.

Westbridge Academy in Grand Rapids, Michigan, started in the late 1960s. It provides middle school and high school dropouts and potential dropouts with an individualized curriculum, counseling, contracting through a token economy, and an array of interest-based curricular offerings. Westbridge has helped thousands of Grand Rapids adolescents to return to school, learn, and graduate.

Expelled/Incarcerated Students: With zero tolerance now established in almost every state and with the increasingly aggressive efforts of police and juvenile authorities, more and more school-age youth are "outside" the regular public schools. However, a growing number of states and school districts now require public schools to have alternatives to expulsion. This is true in Oregon, Texas, and a number of other states.

School districts often create programs for expelled students to ensure that these troubled youth continue to be supervised and educated. Because some expelled youth are so violent and aggressive, some school districts have even established daytime incarceration programs so that parents of these youth can still maintain their daytime jobs without worry for their children's actions. With a massive increase in juvenile offenders, education "inside" the juvenile detention and prison system has become essential.

While these programs cannot provide for volunteer choice, they are developed to address the unique needs of the students being served and often model successful dropout prevention schools. Many of these programs emphasize drug and alcohol education, anger management, and conflict mediation as central themes throughout the academic curriculum.

Alternatives for troubled students also use some type of behavior modification as a key aspect of the program. Some programs use a "point" system, similar to airline frequent flyer programs. Students earn points by coming to school, attending classes, doing their homework, completing lessons and courses, and showing positive behavior. Students may "spend" their points for time in the in-school recreation center, where they can listen to music and play pool and other games; or they can exchange points for coupons for movies, fast food, or music CDs. Often, these programs have "plateaus," where students earn larger and more valuable awards, like a week-long backpacking or rafting trip at the end of the year.

Other programs actually pay students for completing courses satisfactorily. A unique summer program in Boise, Idaho, involves a partnership between the school district and the local private industry council. It pays students $50 per credit during a summer program so that students can earn a total of $250. If students complete all of their courses successfully, they are able to earn an additional $50.

While some educators and citizens are offended by the use of rewards for educational achievement, proponents of this approach maintain that for high-risk, unmotivated, poor students, such programs are well worth the cost.

Motivated and Talented Youth: The most able students in public education often are bored and unchallenged. As a result, many of the brightest students develop behavioral problems and never fulfill their potential. By carefully designing educational programs to capitalize on the skills, abilities, and talents of these students, schools can facilitate truly remarkable learning. Elementary students may be found doing geometry and calculus; high school students may be taking advanced college courses. These schools often involve individualized study and individual and group research projects. They often provide opportunities for students to work with outstanding professionals in the areas that interest them.

Many large city magnet programs and statewide residential alternatives focus on unusually talented and gifted students. A growing number of districts now have performing arts programs for K–12 students, which provide an opportunity for students to work with professional artists. One of the oldest and best-known performing arts schools, once located in New York City, was the focus of the 1980 feature film, *Fame*.

ALTERNATIVES THAT FOCUS ON THEMATIC, CURRICULAR, OR CAREER EMPHASES

At the middle and high school levels, the vast majority of alternative, magnet, and charter schools focus on a special curricular or career theme. These schools have been found to be extremely successful in motivating students toward enhanced academic achievement. The concept is very simple. In addition to the usual requirements for high school graduation, student learning is connected to the academic or professional world. While students still study English, math, history, etc., they relate these courses to a real-world interest or theme. Some will focus their study on radio and television broadcasting, engineering, performing arts, law, international studies, cultural studies, or one of the many health professions. These schools often are situated in the workplace, and students usually study with professionals in their field of interest.

At the elementary level, these schools may emphasize culture and language and teach through the immersion process. Other elementary alternative schools may focus on math and science, the study of the environment, or the performing arts. Hawthorne Elementary School in Seattle focuses its curriculum on the richness of the African-American culture. Through this theme, the faculty, staff, parents, and students join to embrace the primary goal of the school, which is to ensure that all students complete the elementary years with a successful level of student achievement. The school offers a warranty that assures all parents that if they keep their students in school, they will achieve a higher grade level.

Thematic, curricular, and career options at the secondary level are abundant in the Houston Independent School District in Texas, where a student may enroll in high schools for the health professions, law enforcement and criminal justice, performing and visual arts, and many others. Thousands of middle and high school students take advantage of a full menu of alternatives offered throughout the city. (See Chapter Six.)

These programs are growing rapidly because of the dramatic increase in parental interest in choice and smaller, focused schools. They will be discussed in further detail in later sections on charter and magnet schools.

ALTERNATIVES THAT FOCUS ON EXPERIENTIAL LEARNING

Based in part on the ideas of the educational philosopher John Dewey, many alternative schools in the United States emphasize "learning by doing." These schools place a high priority on getting students out of school and away from traditional school environments. Experiential learning programs usually are located in nonschool settings and offer the students opportunities to both attend school and learn in hospitals, radio and television stations, corporations, and a host of small-business settings. These schools-without-walls programs can be found in Seattle, Grand Rapids, Chicago, New York, and many other medium to large urban areas.

The first such alternative school in the country was the Parkway Program of the school district of Philadelphia, established in 1969. Parkway students attend classes in museums, hospitals, libraries, government agencies, banking institutions, and newspapers. Their teachers are curators, biologists, health professionals, librarians, and bankers. Back at their home base, the students work with teachers and staff to meet graduation requirements and discuss their out-of-school learning experiences.

These programs feature extensive real-life practica, internships, and volunteer service projects to enhance learning. Many internship programs place students with business and government leaders so that they can gain experience with top executive decision makers. Technical apprenticeships also provide invaluable training and career preparation for participating students.

Another flourishing model involves creating small businesses operated by students as entrepreneurs. These programs prepare students to learn market analysis, how to create and operate the business, and how to maintain financial accountability. From small student stores to international import and export ventures, these programs and schools teach students the essentials of entrepreneurship through real-life experience. Several national networks and organizations, including Rural Entrepreneurship through Action Learning (REAL) in Athens,

Georgia, and MicroSociety Inc., in Philadelphia, support these programs and schools.

Probably the most well-known program involving out-of-school experience is Foxfire, which originated in Rabun Gap, Georgia. Some 20 years ago, students in Rabun Gap began collecting and writing about the folkways and culture of the rural mountains of eastern Georgia. What started as a student-created, mimeographed newsletter soon grew into a million-dollar business operated and managed by a group of high-risk high school students and their teachers (Wigginton, 1989). Foxfire has established five Teacher Outreach Centers to train teachers in the Foxfire approach and has created 11 Foxfire-affiliated teacher networks in the United States (Smith, 1991).

ALTERNATIVES THAT FOCUS ON SCHOOL ORGANIZATION AND ADMINISTRATION

Some of the most inventive alternative programs involve new and creative ways of organizing and administrating schools. Many alternative schools are organized and operated as year-round schools, others as extended-day programs. Some schools divide the school year into three-week or five-week blocks so that students study a few subjects intensively for a short time. Other alternative schools operate on a university-type schedule, with classes on alternate days. Some alternatives schedule classes Monday through Thursday and give students Friday off if they have successfully completed the week's academic expectations. Other alternatives are late-afternoon and evening programs. Many alternative schools open early in the morning and schedule classes through the evening to accommodate the schedules of the students. Some never close, such as Minnesota's Community Learning Centers, which are available 24 hours a day through electronic access.

Schools within a School: One of the earliest and more popular type of alternative school that focuses on a particular administrative and organizational approach is the "school within a school." At one time, more of these programs were to be found in public education than any other type of alternative.

These alternative schools are housed in the traditional school complex. They are often found at the end of hallways, in secluded wings, or in annex facilities connected to the school. These programs represent all types of alternative models, from free schools to programs for expelled youth. In many cases, an alternative school receives its opportunity to begin through the availability of space in an existing school. Most successful programs eventually move to their own sites within a few years. However, throughout the country, one will find schools within schools, usually at the high school level, that have operated successfully for decades.

Over the past decade, the Coalition of Essential Schools, growing from the early leadership of Ted Sizer at Brown University, has expanded into a major national reform initiative that encourages the school-within-a-school concept. Focusing on secondary schools, the Coalition seeks to renew the comprehensive secondary school model by creating small, autonomous, focused learning environments, quite similar to successful schools within schools.

Cluster Alternatives: There are a few alternatives in the country where the entire school has been broken into clusters of alternatives. For example, the Gem School in Merritt Island, Florida, has four distinct programs operating in one building. Most of these alternatives serve students and parents in a single school district. There are many examples in the country where a single alternative will serve several different school districts, especially in rural and suburban areas. There are a few alternatives serving an entire state, such as Mt. Edgecombe High School, a residential alternative in Sitka, Alaska. This program provides rigorous academic preparation for students from more than 100 small, rural communities throughout the state.

The Houston Independent School District in Texas organized its alternative schools into four basic clusters of offerings. The 200,000-student district is administered by 11 subdistricts, with a 12th alternative district serving the other districts. This alternative district is organized into four clusters of programs by curriculum emphasis, student needs, demographics, and administrative focus. Cluster A schools are magnets; Cluster B schools and programs are for high-risk youth; Cluster C schools and programs serve adjudicated youth; and Cluster D schools provide Graduate Equivalency Diploma (GED) instruction and often operate primarily as contract schools through outside agencies.

Charter Schools: Charter schools represent yet another type of alternative that has restructured the relationship with public education. They are quasi-private schools governed and operated as nonprofit companies. These programs feature shared leadership, multiple corporations overseeing the various functions of the school, and total parent support. Charter schools are discussed more fully in Chapter Seven.

CONCLUSION

In the next chapter, the many decisions that must be made in starting alternative schools will be explored. With the exception, perhaps, of Montessori schools, even the most established type of alternative model can never be replicated "lock, stock, and barrel." Each new alternative school must be crafted and constructed by a particular group of teachers, parents, administrators, and students. Each alternative will be unique and will reflect the distinctive skills, abilities, interests, and philosophies of a particular group of people.

Established alternative models can help shorten and focus the process of developing an alternative program by serving as an advanced organizer for people to consider. They provide schools to visit; material to read; teachers, administrators, and parents to learn from; and a vast storehouse of creative ideas. The goal is not simply to replicate a particular school, but to borrow ideas and models from the wealth of successful programs to create one that will meet student needs.

REFERENCES

Adler, M.A. (1982). *The Paideia proposal.* New York: Macmillan.

Association of Waldorf Schools of North America. (n.d.). [Pamphlet]. Fair Oaks, CA: Author.

Gardner, H. (1983). *Frames of mind.* New York: Basic Books.

Gardner, H. (1989). *To open minds.* New York: Basic Books.

Gardner, H. (1991). *The unschooled mind.* New York: Basic Books.

Kahn, D. (Ed.). (1993). *Montessori in the public schools.* Cleveland: North American Montessori Teachers' Association.

Montessori, M. (1967). *The absorbent mind.* New York: Holt, Rinehart, and Winston.

National School Boards Association. (1989). *An equal chance: Educating at risk children to succeed.* Alexandria, VA: Author.

Neill, A.S. (1977). *Summerhill: A radical approach to child rearing.* New York: Pocket Books.

Rathbone, C. (1971). *Open education.* New York: Citation Press.

Smith, H. (1991). *"Foxfire teacher networks," staff development: New demands, new realities, new perspectives* (2nd ed.). New York: Teachers College Press.

Wigginton, E. (1989, February). Foxfire grows up. *Harvard Educational Review, 59* (1), 24–49.

5

Starting Alternative Schools

If you come to a fork in the road, take it.

Yogi Berra

HERE IS NO SINGLE BEST WAY to start an alternative school. Strategies and processes will vary in every community. There are a variety of issues that must be addressed, a list of decisions that must be made, financial challenges that must be met. Yet thousands of effective alternative schools have been developed over the past 30 years. Their success emanates from the energy and work of committed individuals and groups who are dedicated to providing educational choices and improving schools.

WHO CAN START AN ALTERNATIVE SCHOOL?

Alternative schools can be initiated by almost every possible segment of the community. Surely the easiest way to start or expand alternative schools and programs is for a superintendent or school board to make a decision to create new alternatives. However, history has shown that one determined person or a small group willing to persevere can successfully create a public school alternative. Alternatives have been started by parents, teachers, school administrators, school boards, philanthropic foundations, and even the courts and federal agencies. In each community, alternatives have been developed in quite distinctive ways.

Sometimes it is a group of parents who approach a school board with a proposal, sometimes even a demand, that a particular type of alternative be established. Very determined parents or community leaders may stand for election to local boards of education in order to advocate alternative schools and programs. That is how alternatives were started in St. Paul, Minnesota; Grand Rapids, Michigan; Portland, Oregon; and a host of other communities. The power of an organized group of parents to influence education policy often can be the most expeditious avenue for change.

It is often a group of teachers working in traditional or alternative public schools who organize and start new alternative, magnet, or charter schools. This is what happened in Indianapolis when a group of eight teachers began studying the concept of multiple intelligences. The teachers visited Harvard University and talked with and gained the support of Howard Gardner, an internationally recognized scholar and advocate of the multiple intelligences approach for teaching. The unified efforts of these teachers resulted in the establishment of the Key

Elementary School, based on the theory of multiple intelligences.

Increasingly, as alternative schools have become viewed as a "conservative response to local problems," school administrators and boards of trustees have become proactive in starting and expanding alternative schools, or at least in establishing a policy that permits or encourages the development of alternatives. This approach, while infrequent in practice, may actually be the fastest means of starting or expanding alternative schools and programs (Smith, Barr, & Burke, 1976).

A group of school districts, educational service organizations, or social service agencies often will form a consortium to create a single alternative school serving students from each of the participating school districts. Such consortiums occur throughout the country, usually serving students from neighboring rural areas where individual school districts may lack the resources to create alternative schools.

In a growing number of states, alternative, magnet, and charter schools have been mandated or encouraged through legislation. Many state legislatures provide incentive funding for programs that serve at-risk youth. Others require districts to create and operate alternative schools, and more than 23 states now have charter school legislation in place to foster the development of that option.

Many of the complex urban magnet programs were created as a result of court orders. During the 1970s and 1980s, and occasionally even in the 1990s, federal courts mandated the creation of "volunteer choice" magnet schools as part of districtwide desegregation plans. Over the years, court-ordered magnet programs have been designated as the most positive aspect of school desegregation programs, whether the city is Kansas City, Milwaukee, Louisville, or South Boston.

For years, federal agencies and state departments of education have provided funding to encourage the development and support of alternative, magnet, and charter schools. Most recently, the U.S. Department of Education has offered block grants to enable the creation of charter schools. In Alaska, the state department of education created an alternative high school, Mt. Edgecombe School, for the entire state.

A growing number of community colleges in Oregon, California, and elsewhere have created alternative programs both to meet a community need and to provide a bridge for students to higher education. Several state universities (University of North Carolina, Louisiana State University, and Ball State University, as well as community colleges in Oregon, California, New Jersey, and others) operate alternative schools as learning laboratories for colleges of education, serving both local and state populations (Kellmayer, 1995).

For years, philanthropists and foundations have channeled millions of dollars to public education to foster the development of alternative schools and programs designed to serve a variety of youth whose needs are not met in traditional public schools. The Parkway School in Philadelphia, one of the nation's first alternative schools, was started with support from the Ford Foundation. Hundreds of other foundations continue to place education, the creation of alternative approaches, innovation, and youth at risk as their top funding priorities.

Occasionally, it is even a group of articulate, assertive students who become the force for starting an alternative. In recent years, business and professional leaders also have been instrumental in creating career academies, magnet schools, and charter schools. A number of new alternative schools are managed as private enterprises on a contract basis (Young, 1990).

Whether it is a federal court, a state legislature, a super-intendent or local board of trustees, or an individual or group, the issues that must be dealt with are basically the same. Regardless of where the initiative starts for the creation of an alternative, there are essential issues that must be addressed. However, there are some particular issues that need to be addressed separately by those outside the existing school structure and by school administrators.

INITIAL STEPS FOR INDIVIDUALS AND GROUPS

While it is more difficult for an individual or group outside the existing school structure to initiate an alternative school, there are legions of good examples to impress even the most timid observer that it can be done and done well, even in an adversarial situation. Those outside the education structure need to take the following steps:

Check out the law and state regulations. The first step in the creation or expansion of an alternative school is to analyze the lay of the land regarding the political climate. A quick first step is to contact the local or state superintendent of schools and request information regarding policies that relate to alternative schools and the types of alternatives that are currently available or mandated in a school district or a state. It is important to learn about state legislation that affects alternatives. Does the state require certain types of alternatives? Has the state passed charter school legislation? Does the state provide incentive funding for the creation of certain types of alternatives? How are alternatives perceived at the state and local levels? Copies of legislation regarding alternative schools, or school district policies regarding alternatives, should be obtained in order to understand the exact nature and specifics of the policy and legislation. There are vast differences in charter school legislation. Some states have provided for little more than "site-based management" under the guise of the charter school rubric. Other states require and provide incentive funding only for at-risk programs and sometimes only as alternatives to expulsion or alternatives for dropouts.

> *I thought I would check out the political situation. I called the State Superintendent of Schools office and asked about alternative schools and charter schools. His secretary said, "He'll get back to you." That was three months ago. Then I finally called the local superintendent's office here in my school district. Unfortunately, he was right to the point. All he said was, "No way. We believe in neighborhood schools."*

Parent, western state

A review of the political situation may turn up a very positive environment for the creation or expansion of alternatives. It also may reveal that there are no policies nor funding incentives and that the idea of alternatives is perceived with grave suspicion.

Seek allies. A number of states have strong, long-standing professional organizations that support alternative public schools. In some states, these organizations are just loose networks of people who are interested in and support alternatives. The stronger the state organization, the more complex and established the state's alternative schools tend to be. (See Appendix III for alternative school support associations.)

If the state has an alternative school/charter school professional association or contact people, this will prove to be the best source of information regarding state and school district interest, responsiveness, and policy and legislation. The state association also can help assess the political climate and can provide consultation and advice.

While access to a state association is helpful, it is often a local, informal network of parents, educators, and concerned citizens that can provide immediate support and assistance. Most communities have individuals sympathetic to the need for alternative schools. Connecting with them often requires a surprisingly small amount of time and effort. Parent groups, local educators, bulletin boards—both manual and electronic—the media, church organizations, social service providers, and perhaps next-door neighbors may be the connection to supportive allies.

> *Technology is amazing. I dialed into the local community college electronic bulletin board and, immediately, I found a dozen people who wanted to create an alternative school. We're now meeting and planning our proposal.*
>
> Parent, Texas

Building a sense of community in an emerging program is vital to its success. Models of this approach are readily available and should be considered by any group working to create an alternative school.

Anticipate the dark side of alternative education politics. While there are many areas of the country where a positive, supportive atmosphere can be found for the development or expansion of alternative and charter schools, advocates often can expect a negative, even hostile response in some communities. Even those who support alternative schools may do it for selfish motives. Some may want to move disruptive students out of public schools to a detention center. Some school leaders will want some type of alternative to expulsion with little regard for program quality, simply so the school district can receive the average daily financial support from the state. Some charter school proponents may be "private schoolers" or "home schoolers" attempting to have their own program supported by state dollars. Some politicians may promote charter schools only to advance an agenda of giving tax credits to private school parents. Others may truly believe that a significant number of youth, often poor and minority students, should not be permitted the opportunity to attend school with "their children." Despite the success of alternative schools, some individuals' motives for support may have little to do with establishing effective schools for all children. Thus it is prudent advice for anyone seeking to create an alternative school to keep a keen eye toward a sponsor's motive.

INITIAL STEPS FOR SCHOOL DISTRICTS

For school districts interested in creating or expanding alternative schools, the process usually is very different. Most districts in the nation now operate at least one alternative program. Yet few districts acknowledge having developed a sufficient number of programs to have met the challenge of successfully educating the community's youth. Whether creating or expanding schools, assessing need and gaining public support are imperative.

Community surveys. A community survey is an invaluable means of assessing interest and support in starting alternatives and magnet schools. Some school districts have successfully used complex, multi-page surveys to assess support, while others have raised a single question with patrons, such as, "Would you and your children be interested in attending a year-round school outside your own neighborhood if transportation were provided?" If 200 or more parents indicate their interest, serious planning can begin.

Medium to large school districts often send out parent surveys describing different types of alternatives. Such surveys often lead to clusters of support for particular schools and provide demographic data on areas of strongest support. Some community surveys appear as supplements in the local newspaper, while others are sent home with students. Local TV and radio stations may provide assistance in community survey and awareness campaigns.

School/community forums. Many alternative schools have grown out of school/community forums. Whether the forums are organized by the superintendent, the mayor, or community groups, the process is almost always the same. From a cross-section of school, community, business, and government, leaders are invited to a meeting to discuss community issues. Representatives usually include teachers, administrators, parents, business leaders, commissioners, city council members, newspaper editors and publishers, school board members, and police. The forum can focus on a specific problem or a group of problems, such as gangs, violence, teen pregnancy, dropouts, and unemployment. The forum also can involve a much broader discussion of future growth and quality of life.

While forums can be very informal discussions, there are a number of more formal models that have been used effectively. Two such models are the Kellogg Foundation Community Forum and the United States Extension Service Community Action Forum. Each of these models provides for comprehensive community involvement and interaction resulting in the development of an action plan. Regardless of how the forum is organized, the idea is to bring together school, community, and government leaders to solve problems and enhance opportunities for all youth. Alternative schools often will emerge as a rational response to a variety of community problems.

School district planning teams. School districts that set out to diversify the entire community's educational program through the creation of a number of alternative schools usually convene a district planning team, often composed of teachers, administrators, and parents from every school in the district. Such large planning efforts budget for planning and development; and they use consultants, travel to other cities to visit alternative schools, and conduct exhaustive literature reviews for information and research about different types of alternatives.

- **Administrative fiat.** Some school districts simply announce that one or more public schools in the community will be replaced by new alternative schools. When this happens, all students, parents, teachers, and administrators must choose a new program that they wish to attend. This often is viewed as a rather harsh, heavy-handed approach to school reform and often generates considerable anxiety, frustration, and anger. The advantage, of course, is that no one can simply stay where they are and do what they have been doing. Everyone has to select a new program. This approach has been used in Texas in both San Antonio and Corpus Christi.

- **Evolution.** Sometimes the most politically effective avenue for creating new programs is to support and nurture a menu of offerings and allow them to evolve. The Vancouver School District in Washington used a five-year planning and development strategy to create clusters of alternatives in each of the district's four high schools. These clusters include such alternatives as the International High School Baccalaureate Degree program; Eagle's Wing, an interdisciplinary self-directed study option; Pan Terra, a dropout prevention program; extended class periods for greater in-depth study, and a variety of career academies. While Vancouver's approach has taken a considerable amount of time and expense, school leaders believe that their approach will yield long-term, positive change.

BE PREPARED FOR PROBLEMS

While alternative schools have almost universally been accepted as an essential part of any school district's effort to educate all students, they often are still viewed with a blend of suspicion and distrust. In a landmark study of 14 alternative schools and programs for at-risk youth, Wehlage and his colleagues (1989) at the University of Wisconsin, Madison, concluded:

> *In some communities . . . alternative schools are considered illegitimate by the profession and the public. Often this perception of illegitimacy can make it difficult, if not impossible for these programs to carry out the important function of offering high-quality programs to students and providing leadership and innovation* (p. 222).

This suspicion can be a result of several factors. First, many alternatives have been so successful at educating at-risk youth that traditional educators assume that these special schools are watering down their curriculum and standards. Too often, traditional educators believe that no one can educate these youth. And because alternative schools use a wide range of innovative and experimental techniques, conventional school educators may feel there is an implicit criticism of their approach and their practices.

Another problem is that effective alternative schools almost always attract attention. The local media will report graduation ceremonies, special projects, and novel learning experiences. Reporters seem especially interested in recording the innovative, creative learning experiences that typify alternative schools and that are different from those in conventional schools. And the media love to report positive, heartwarming stories about high-risk kids who are "doing well." Thus effective alternative schools begin to attract regional and national attention. This type of attention inevitably inspires jealousy and criticism from others in a district.

In addition to suspicion and jealousy, alternative schools also can suffer from the motives and misconceptions of some of those who support the concept. Too often, teachers, administrators, and counselors see the development of an alternative school as an opportunity to try to purge their schools of the most difficult, disruptive, and emotionally disturbed students. Some school districts may see alternative schools as a new and sophisticated student tracking system. It is for this reason that those who develop alternative schools often focus on "approaches to learning," rather than certain types of students, and work to attract a heterogeneous cross-section of students.

Whenever alternative schools are started, there inevitably is confusion among many of the people who support the concept. Some teachers who support the development of a particular alternative school and who choose to teach in that school may discover that what they thought they would enjoy proves to be intolerable. Students and parents may also feel drawn to an alternative school only to discover that the adjustment to "self-directed learning," for example, turns out to be very, very difficult. Concise orientations, cooperative staff development, and regular opportunities to meet and talk need to be provided for teachers, students, and their parents so that everyone understands to the best of their ability the challenges that are before them.

School districts also will have difficulties accommodating highly innovative alternative schools within existing state and local regulations and policies. The greatest problem often is trying to relate interdisciplinary and nontraditional study to typical high school graduation requirements. Other state and local regulations and policies, which govern everything from transportation schedules to the number of books in the library, often pose insurmountable problems to highly innovative alternative schools, especially those schools that are housed in an unusual community facility. Mediating between state and district policies and effective practice in alternative programs will always be a challenge to school and district educators.

STRATEGIES FOR STARTING AN ALTERNATIVE PUBLIC SCHOOL

Starting an alternative school has become easier during recent years. Originally, many alternative schools were started by small groups of activists who organized political campaigns to force school boards to allow them to create a new school that reflected their particular interest or philosophy. As more and more alternative schools have been developed, evaluated, and researched, the schools have become more acceptable and easier to implement. This is due in part to the work of the professional associations of alternative schools mentioned earlier, who have lobbied successfully with legislators, state departments of education, and local school boards to support the concept. School districts increasingly are required by states to develop alternative schools and programs as a safety net for dropouts, and many states provide special funding formulas to support the development and maintenance of alternative schools. Many school districts also have developed enabling policies that provide an established process for groups to propose new alternative public schools, so that over time these communities will offer an increased variety of learning opportunities for parents and students (Barr & Parrett, 1995).

While no two alternative public schools are started in the same way, there are a number of steps that are almost always present in the process.

Develop a rationale. Regardless of who initiates an alternative school, one of the initial tasks that must be completed is to develop a strong rationale. In creating a new alternative school, a number of different rationales might be used:

- **Address a problem.** One of the best ways to ensure the approval of a new alternative school or program is to demonstrate how the new program would address a troubling problem or concern in the community. Often communities and schools may mobilize to address such problems as crime, gangs, dropouts, or even the students who will not go to a four-year college. Because alternative schools have such a proven track record of alleviating so many of the problems that confront schools and communities, there is no better place to start the creation of an alternative than with a real community concern. This also provides a very simple and effective way to evaluate and assess the effectiveness of the alternative over time in addressing the identified problem.

- **Meet the needs and interests of students.** In addition to proposing a new alternative as a solution to a particular problem, a strong rationale can be established for developing programs that better address the needs and interests of students. This might include the development of a more effective instructional approach, such as individualized study and project work. It might focus on developing a program aimed at a particular teaching/learning style, such as an emphasis on multiple intelligences. Other types of alternatives might focus on particular occupations or on developing a particular talent, such as the arts.

- **Take advantage of unusual opportunities.** Some alternative schools are proposed to build upon a unique characteristic of the community. In Philadelphia, the idea was to develop a "school without walls" that capitalized on the city's cultural and business resources. In more rural areas, the focus might be developing access to rich cultural folklore. In Los Angeles, magnet schools were developed to take advantage of the television and motion picture industry; in Houston, alternatives were developed in cooperation with the petrochemical industry and health professions.

- **Provide special services.** Some alternative schools have been developed that provide a nontraditional or distinctive service to parents and students, such as year-round schools. It is all but impossible to transform a neighborhood school into a year-round program, but an alternative year-round school will attract parents from throughout the district. Extended-day schools that assure working parents that their children are in a safe, supervised, and stimulating atmosphere are popular alternatives. The development of an evening program or a graduation equivalency program will enable youth and adults who dropped out of school or who were never able to finish school to complete their education.

- **Reform and restructure.** Some alternative schools are used as pilot projects for proposed education reforms. Alternatives have been created in order to implement nongraded or multi-age classrooms, major enhancements of technology, interdisciplinary-studies academies, tech-prep programs, and a host of others. A growing number of educators, legislators, and parents see alternatives as the best means to quickly and effectively implement a wide variety of reforms in public education.

Build consensus. It is absolutely essential to build consensus when creating an alternative school. The process must include teachers, parents, and even students who share particular beliefs or concerns. Increasingly, district administrators or school board members convene planning groups, often providing financial support to facilitate the group's work. Parents can be extremely helpful and influential in these groups, especially when they are helping to develop a school that can serve their own children. Successful local planning may depend on building a consensus among these constituencies.

Develop a preliminary proposal. Out of the consensus-building phase, a preliminary proposal should be developed that includes a rationale, philosophy, the problem(s) to be addressed, overall school goals and objectives, a general statement regarding the teaching and learning approach, curriculum to be emphasized, type of students to be served, timeline, budget, and a recommendation for evaluation. The task of developing the preliminary proposal is in itself part of the consensus-building process, for it requires a group to assemble their ideas and beliefs into a written plan.

Seek authorization and approval. Experience has taught that a group seeking to develop an alternative public school usually should not seek board approval at their initial presentation. Rather, the board should be approached on at least two or three different occasions. The first time provides a briefing and information session for the board that informs the board of the group's rationale and purpose. Next, the group might present a preliminary proposal or concept paper and seek board approval for an official planning process to study the issue and make recommendations.

At the first or second board appearance, the group may ask education consultants, teachers, administrators, students, or parents from an existing alternative school to help provide information to the board and to answer questions. Only after a school board has developed a receptive attitude toward the alternative school and has encouraged further exploration of the concept should the board be presented with a full proposal and asked to approve the establishment of an alternative school. Obviously, it can be invaluable to include supportive individual board members in the planning process.

Select teachers and administrators. Frequently, the teachers and administrators who plan and develop the alternative school are also the majority of faculty who will be teaching in the new program. For this reason, the preliminary planning team must include any interested teachers and administrators from the district. Furthermore, it is absolutely essential that the preliminary planning group actively participate in the final selection of teachers and administrators for the school.

The district should inform potential teachers and administrators of the effort and encourage those interested to learn about the alternative school concept and the development of the school. This process often will identify district teachers who have had extensive training or experience in exactly the type of alternative that is being developed. For example, when the Indianapolis School District was planning a new Montessori alternative elementary school, the board worried that the time and cost of training teachers in the Montessori approach might be prohibitive. A districtwide survey discovered that there were more than 20 elementary teachers in the Indianapolis public schools who already were certified Montessori teachers and were quite excited about joining the planning group and having an opportunity to teach in the new Montessori alternative.

Choosing a leader for the school is perhaps the most critical element in the staffing process. While many programs have effectively started through the traditional approach of first selecting the principal and charging that individual with subsequent staffing duties, more than a few programs have suffered, even failed, due to choosing the "wrong" person to lead the school. The odds of locating a successful leader are far higher if the planning group, composed of teachers and parents who will be a part of the school, is intimately involved in the process.

Approve a process for planning and development. The planning process is extremely important to the creation of an alternative school. It is a time when the new school is conceptualized and designed. For many parents, teachers, administrators, and students, this is an exciting opportunity to design the school of their dreams, their own ideal school.

While it is important that there is adequate time for planning, there can be a danger in having too much time for planning. More than one school district has approved a study group and subsequently required a two-year planning schedule in the hope that the group will plan the program to death. Successful alternative schools should not take more than a year to plan. There is only so much that can be accomplished before the school is open, and a shorter planning and implementation schedule leads to maximum participation, enthusiasm, and commitment.

Once the school has opened its doors, continued planning and staff development should include visits to other schools, not to simply replicate what is found but for teachers, administrators, and parents of the new school to develop networks and learn from experienced veterans of successful alternative schools. During the first summer after the alternative school has opened, the faculty should have sufficient time to revise curricula, participate in further staff development and training, and re-evaluate the school's effectiveness. Funding the planning and development process will require modest support to provide for summer contracts, travel to other schools, consultants for staff development, equipping the facility, and a variety of start-up costs.

Select a facility. Alternative schools often are located in small, abandoned school facilities, in an isolated corridor of an existing school, or in leased facilities in the community. Alternative schools have been started in churches, warehouses, former bank buildings, hotels, gas stations, and almost anywhere an empty retail or office building is available. Magnet schools, which usually are housed in a facility that relates to a particular curriculum focus, can be found in hospitals, aircraft hangers, shopping malls, theaters, and even at the city zoo. For at-risk youth, who often possess negative attitudes toward school, an off-campus location has many advantages and may be critical to the school's success. One superb location for an at-risk alternative high school is at or near a community college or some other postsecondary institution. Whatever the facility and location, care needs to be taken in advance to ensure that appropriate transportation services and parking facilities are available and that the facility meets state and local building, fire, and health codes for schools.

Market the program. Once formally approved, seek the school district's help to inform the community of the new education option. It is critical to have the new school included in districtwide communications and brochures. Get on the district Web page or create a new one for the alternative school. Television and radio talk shows, electronic bulletin boards, booths at local fairs and events, and T-shirts represent a few of the many marketing strategies successfully used by new alternative programs. Perhaps the best approach is through personal contact. Make certain that district public representatives, administrators, and school counselors and advisors have detailed information on the program.

And do not overlook the students and parents who have contributed to the development of the school's creation. These folks, mainly through word of mouth, will spread the word.

Enroll students. After the enrollment cap has been set and the parameters for categories of students have been determined, a careful process of marketing, recruitment, selection, and enrollment must occur. This usually includes school district communication, newspaper articles, and media announcements. It often begins with information and orientation sessions for all building principals and counselors, open community meetings for students and parents, and many informal contacts. During the application period, the school or district should provide help sessions. Then personal interviews usually are held with students and their parents. Some programs with a particular focus, such as performing arts or advanced technology, may require auditions, portfolios, or a demonstration of minimal skills.

It is essential that the faculty of the alternative school have responsibility for enrolling students based on the approved criteria and procedures. Successful alternative schools also require a written commitment or contract from the parent and student, which acknowledges an understanding of the program and its expectations for students and parents.

Even though the alternative program should be available to students and parents on the basis of personal choice, alternative schools can ensure a diversified student body by establishing quotas. Many schools establish a lottery process because of the high number of applicants, and they make an effort to enroll a student population that reflects their community. Through this process, a school can provide for ethnic, economic, age, and gender balance and avoid the negative connotation of serving only at-risk students.

Institute shared decision making. Shared decision making is as essential to effective alternative programs as is school choice. The school decision-making process should grow out of the planning process and include a carefully planned school management team, which involves parents, students, and teachers. Successful alternative schools will provide a range of models of governance and decision making to guide a new program.

Following these steps, most successful alternative schools have accomplished their initial goal of effectively starting their program. Making it work becomes the consuming challenge for all involved as the hard work of design and organization quickly fades into the past.

COMPONENTS FOR SUCCESS IN AN ALTERNATIVE PUBLIC SCHOOL

After almost 30 years of experience, a number of components have been identified that are crucial to the success of a new alternative school.

Use existing school district funds. To be successful, alternative schools should be funded by the local school district in the same way as all other schools. The alternative school should function within the existing per-pupil cost based on the established pupil-teacher ratio in a school district. This means each alternative school will be staffed on the basis of student enrollment at other schools. Extra funding for start-up expenses also must be addressed.

Many states provide a differential formula to support the increased costs associated with teaching high-risk youth. However, alternative schools funded solely by external grants often do not survive once the grant expires.

Start small, but not too small. Compared to other public schools, alternative schools are always relatively small. This is clearly one of the reasons that they have been so successful. Unfortunately, decisions often are made to start an alternative school as a pilot project or in some other small way and then to expand later.

To be successful, alternative schools should begin with a sufficient number of students to justify at least four teachers. With a careful selection of the four teachers, most of the required curriculum can be addressed. With fewer teachers, the school program will place unreasonable demands on the faculty and often will force students to rely on other schools to meet graduation requirements. This can reduce the alternative school to only a part-time program. For maximum success with at-risk youth, alternative schools should provide as much of a total education program as possible. Most successful alternative programs cap enrollments at 150 to 300 students.

Another approach to creating an alternative school is adding a grade per year. Some schools have started with the ninth grade and have added the next grade each year until an entire high school program is in place.

Use teachers from the school district. To be successful, alternative schools should be a home-grown product. While it might be good to recruit a few teachers with unique experience from outside the community, the school should be planned, developed, and operated by teachers, parents, and administrators from within the district. In fact, alternative schools often recruit some of the most respected teachers in a school district for their expertise. It is also vital that a core of teachers who will teach in the alternative school be involved in the district and community team that plans the program.

Alternative schools should be as autonomous as possible. Administratively, this means the alternative school should have a principal or head teacher who reports in exactly the same manner as any other building principal in the school district. Educationally, this means that the alternative school should have as much freedom as possible from rules and regulations and be evaluated on the performance outcomes of the students. Most states have policies that permit schools to apply for a waiver of administrative rules governing public education if they replace them with an alternate plan.

Alternative schools must document their effectiveness. Each alternative public school should develop a process and product evaluation plan, as well as a comprehensive menu of student assessment measures to demonstrate effectiveness, identify problems and needs, and provide a basis for making necessary adjustments.

Alternative public schools pioneered the use of performance outcomes by requiring graduation competencies, rather than required courses, and likewise were among the first public schools to routinely assess and report student attitudes and behavioral outcomes, as well as achievement scores. Alternative schools also provided the proving grounds for many of the concepts and components of authentic assessment. Narrative evaluations, student portfolios, student-led conferencing, and competency demonstrations represent a sample of these techniques, which increasingly are being used in conventional schools. Many alternative schools also regularly conduct long-term follow-up evaluations of their former students.

Seek long-term commitments. Boards of education should provide a three- to five-year commitment to any alternative school that is approved. It takes three years to document improved achievement and as many as five to seven years to truly establish any new educational program. While alternative schools should have a positive effect on student achievement much sooner than existing schools that are involved in a restructuring or improvement effort, it is unreasonable for school districts or school boards to judge the potential or effectiveness of an alternative program too soon. Some evaluations have been required at the end of the first semester or the first year, which is far too early to effectively assess program success. It is essential that alternative schools have sufficient time to have an adequate effect on students and to develop the most appropriate process of evaluation and documentation.

Create time for staff interaction and development. A hallmark of effective alternative schools is a creative schedule that provides for the blend of necessary academic work, staff planning and interaction, and professional development. While most conventional public schools languish due to suffocating schedules, ill-planned professional development activities and opportunities, and a chronic lack of time each day for collegial interaction, their alternative counterparts flourish, in part, because they have addressed these critical needs.

Do not expand too rapidly. Large urban school districts often will establish large numbers of alternative or magnet programs at one time. Recently, New York approved more than 30 "New Vision" schools that were started almost immediately with little or no opportunity for the teachers in the new schools to have time to plan and develop together. In fact, the teachers in the new schools had little time even to meet one another. When students arrived, some of the schools were almost in chaos.

CONCLUSION

Do our kids appreciate this school? Let me describe a recent event. It was late Friday. I was on the way out when the phone rang. The last thing I wanted was another call, another problem. Everyone else was gone.... I thought about letting the answering machine take it ... but I answered; and was I glad I did. One of

our seniors, who had left during the year to [live] on the East Coast in a more stable family situation, was on the line. He was graduating on schedule and had just been hired in an electrician training program. He was calling to ask if he could list our school as the beneficiary of his newly acquired life insurance policy. Can you believe that? I cried.

Principal, Alternative School
West Coast

How an alternative school is started may well be the most critical aspect of the emerging life and chance for success a new program experiences. Careful and thorough planning, widespread community involvement, attention to district policy, effective marketing, assembling leadership and staffing, and equitable enrollment of students will allow a new school to grow from a healthy start. Rushed openings, inadequate planning, improper enrollment practices, and a host of other potential pitfalls could prove severely damaging or fatal to an emerging school. It is essential that creators of new schools carefully address these and other issues. Starting an alternative school may well be the most challenging adventure of one's career. Do it well, as many communities have learned, and remarkable educational opportunities will appear.

REFERENCES

Barr, R.D., & Parrett, W.H. (1995). *Hope at last for at-risk youth.* Boston: Allyn & Bacon.

Kellmayer, J. (1995). *How to establish an alternative school.* Thousand Oaks, CA: Corwin Press.

Smith, V., Barr, R.D., & Burke, D. (1976). *Alternatives in education.* Bloomington, IN: Phi Delta Kappa.

Wehlage, G.G., Rutter, R.A., Smith, G.A., Lesko, N., & Fernandez, R.R. (1989). *Reducing the risk: Schools as communities of support.* Philadelphia: Falmer Press.

Young, T. (1990). *Public alternative education.* New York: Teachers College Press.

Magnet Schools

Magnet schools? I don't know what you're talking about. What in the world is a magnet school?

Parent, Dallas, Texas, 1980

MAGNET SCHOOLS WERE BORN amid the seething political strife and violence that accompanied school desegregation in the United States during the 1960s. To somehow soften the antagonisms of desegregation, school districts and federal judges began developing a few schools of choice in the hope that they would serve as "magnets" to attract both white and minority parents to voluntarily attend integrated schools. Many parents were given the choice of being "forced bused" to an alien, often violent neighborhood across town or volunteering to attend one of the new "special theme" magnet schools. One overriding goal of the first magnet schools was to slow the "white flight" to the suburbs that always seemed to accompany school desegregation.

During the 1970s, research and evaluation began to identify magnet schools as one of the most promising remedies for helping to alleviate the problems of segregation (McMillan, 1977). Students of diverse backgrounds viewed the opportunity to participate voluntarily in exciting new programs as an attractive alternative to arbitrary forced busing, and this option softened the impact of court-ordered desegregation. Some creative school districts began developing magnet schools to avoid or deflect judicial mandates to desegregate before those mandates were given.

First conceived as little more than a political quick fix to pacify parents, especially white middle-class parents who were being compelled by federal judges to bus their children to racially mixed schools, the concept has matured and evolved to become one of the most impressive success stories in large urban and middle-sized school districts across the nation. Today, magnet schools involve hundreds of districts and more than 4,000 individual schools (Magnet Schools of America, 1996). Some of the large urban school districts (Houston, Louisville, Los Angeles) have developed dozens of these schools and programs supported by complex administrative, transportation, and student-selection systems. Magnet schools, while continuing to provide successful approaches to desegregation, have become some of the most creative, effective schools in America.

In recent years, almost every urban school district in the United States has used magnet schools to diversify the educational program and to offer parents, teachers, and students a remarkable range of choices. Many school districts have as many as 5% to 20% of the entire student population in some type of magnet school, alternative school, or at-risk center.

Modern magnets emphasize specific careers, professions, the arts, the environment, and other themes, as well as the usual requirements for high school graduation. These new magnet schools now integrate both school requirements and career requirements, as well as achieving desegregated student bodies.

Research conducted on magnet schools has been thorough and has yielded extremely positive results. Numerous studies complement thousands of magnet school evaluations over the past two decades to show that student achievement has been extremely impressive, often better than in comprehensive public schools and elite private schools ("Students learn more in magnets," 1996). What is equally important, magnet schools have developed and proven successful in the most demanding public school arena—the large, poor, culturally diverse metropolitan areas of America. All indications today point to one conclusion: magnet schools work.

THE EVOLUTION OF THE MAGNET CONCEPT

While desegregation clearly was the primary motive for developing the early magnet schools, there are other factors that have contributed to their popularity. For example, these schools also have been viewed as a competitive response to urban decline. As large numbers of urban Americans, including middle-class minorities and whites, have abandoned cities and urban schools in favor of suburban public schools and private and parochial schools, many urban school boards have looked to magnet schools to offset this migration. Magnet schools offer nearly everything the private academy or parochial school has to offer, without tuition. In fact, some magnet schools resemble "elite, private academies" within public education. These "elite" public schools help retain middle-class families in urban public schools, as well as offer choices to the conventional public school. Kennedy Elementary School, a Montessori magnet school in Louisville, Kentucky, is located between two major housing projects. Despite its location, the school draws students from all areas of Louisville, and parents vie to get their children enrolled in this award-winning, "low income" neighborhood school (Jefferson County Public Schools, 1995). St. Louis, Milwaukee, and San Diego have implemented regional "magnetization" in an effort to bring suburban school districts into a regional magnet program.

Parents also have contributed significantly to the development of magnet schools. Public school parents have become increasingly more sophisticated consumers of education, demanding competency tests, effective instruction in the basics, enhanced opportunities for participation with the real world, and greater variety in school programs. Magnet schools have provided school boards and administrators with an effective response to these diverse demands.

Magnet schools also encourage business and community groups to participate in public education in new ways. For example, school-to-work partnerships, adopt-a-school initiatives, and business/education roundtable programs have brought the human and financial resources of the business community to districts and individual schools. Often it is the Chamber of Commerce that generates support for business-oriented magnet schools. In Houston, magnet schools are located in the Baylor Medical Center and the World Trade Center and take advantage of the resources of these unique sites. In Los Angeles, magnet schools are located in area radio and television stations. In Dallas, the city's largest magnet school, Skyline Center, is located in an airport hanger.

This combined support of business and education has been a powerful force in revitalizing both schools and urban areas. It provides relevant curriculum and real-world experiences for students. And by carefully placing new magnet schools in declining areas, school districts have contributed tangibly to improving neglected neighborhoods.

One result of these business/education partnerships is the development of magnet schools that focus on specific careers and professions. So successful have these new magnet schools become that the term "magnet school" has shifted significantly from describing a "desegregation school" to describing a school that emphasizes a particular career focus or profession. Today, magnet schools feature petrochemical engineering, health professions, performing arts, law enforcement and criminal justice, radio and television broadcasting, retail merchandising, animal and biological sciences, fashion careers and design, environmental studies, multiple aspects of technology, international studies, law and public service, medical careers, and even teaching profession schools.

For students who are bored, burned out, or antagonized by public education, the opportunity to attend school in a nontraditional setting is often a most welcomed and positive experience. To participate and succeed, students must adjust their behavior, dress, and attitudes to the workplace. As a result, students in these schools are often more motivated, develop a better work ethic, and appear to be more responsible than their counterparts in conventional schools. The culture of the workplace also provides a clear, understandable connection between the importance of learning and performance.

With the growing success of magnet schools, many school districts began to develop them in large numbers throughout their communities. For the first time, alternative schools were not limited to only a single program in a community. Suddenly, magnet schools were beginning to attract a significant percentage of all students in the school district. Today, districtwide magnet offerings often include a variety of schools with different names in diverse locations, all available by choice. The following offerings may characterize a district's "menu" of programs:

- *Alternative Schools:* The term "alternative school" usually is used to describe a program that focuses on a different approach to learning, such as a Montessori school, open school, school without walls, or nongraded school.

- *Magnet Schools:* Magnet schools typically are schools with an academic, career, or professional theme that maintain heterogeneous student populations.

- *Alternative Schools for Suspended Students:* School districts now suspend more students from regular programs, but they offer high-security alternatives. Often these programs are conducted in cooperation with police or juvenile justice authorities.

- *Alternative Schools for Incarcerated Youth:* With more and more young people being convicted of crimes and sentenced to juvenile detention centers, work camps, and prisons, school districts often are providing special alternative schools within correctional facilities for incarcerated youth.

- *Programs of Choice/Schools Within Schools:* School districts may have a wide variety of alternatives housed within a conventional school but available as districtwide options. These schools within schools often are referred to as optional programs or schools of choice. Such programs can include classical schools, fine arts high schools, regional gifted/talented centers, and many others.

- *Conventional Schools:* With large numbers of alternative schools and programs available, most urban school districts emphasize that the conventional or neighborhood schools are now, in fact, one of the community's options.

- *Contract Schools:* Districts in Chelsea, Massachusetts; Hartford, Connecticut; Wichita, Kansas; and St. Clemews, Hawaii, actually contract out the administration of public education to universities or private firms. To date, these experiments appear to work at least as well as previous traditional efforts, and several claim to be much better.

CHALLENGES FACING MAGNET SCHOOLS

In spite of the success and the growing number of magnet schools in the country, there are a number of challenges associated with magnet schools that must be addressed:

Do magnet schools cost more? Because of the emphasis on careers and professions, most magnet schools do have initial costs that far exceed those of other public schools. Most of these costs are associated with specialized equipment and facility updating. Yet with more and more magnet schools being part of adopt-a-school programs and business partnerships, many of these costs have been borne by local businesses. Also, as indicated earlier, many magnet schools are actually located in a particular business or professional setting, which allows for dual use of specialized equipment and facilities. Some districts have initiated effective magnet schools with no more than the standard per-pupil expenditures, thanks to special support from local business, industry, or professions.

However, even with these other sources of funds, creating a magnet school often requires additional funding. For example, when the Houston Public Schools first started magnet schools, they invested $10 million to develop 43 magnet schools. When Milwaukee started its successful "magnet only" plan, they invested $3.3 million to develop 27 new magnet schools. Developing magnet schools is almost always an expensive endeavor, at least in the beginning.

Because of these costs, magnet schools have been challenged for financial inequality. Indeed, serious problems of discrimination and equity are raised in any district where there is a significant difference between the per-pupil expenditures in magnet and conventional schools.

Can magnet schools attract diverse youth? When magnets were first developed in the 1970s, there was considerable concern that these special schools would serve only elite, talented, and usually white, middle-class students. However, most magnet schools use lottery and quota systems to ensure that each school has a culturally diverse student body. In Louisville, Kentucky, for example, each magnet school must achieve established standards (quotas) for cultural diversity, male/female ratios, and appropriate income/economic distribution to represent all families in the community (Strickland, 1996). Many have described magnet schools in communities like Louisville as some of the most heterogeneous schools in America.

Educators have worried about possible ethical problems in making a magnet school so special, so unique, and so exciting that middle-class, Caucasian families would be willing to attend racially mixed schools. As Gordon Foster, former superintendent of schools in Oakland, California, said, "The magnet concept is a message to the white community which says, in effect, this is a school which has been made so attractive . . . you'll want to enroll your child voluntarily in spite of the fact that he will have to go to school with blacks" (McMillan, 1980, p. 18). Charles McMillan

(1980) writes, "If magnets are to prove their worth as a desegregation remedy, they must demonstrate first and foremost their ability to educate a minority child and the poor child whose rights have been denied" (p. 18). The good news is that magnet schools have a demonstrated track record of success in educating all kinds of students and of doing it better than traditional public schools or private schools.

Do magnets produce a brain drain from comprehensive schools? Another concern of many urban educators is that magnet schools act as a "brain drain" to skim off the district's top students, thus unfairly affecting all other schools in the district. Magnets, these critics fear, may deny the minority community its best students and thus further "ghettoize" the black community. Most educators agree that to some degree magnets do "skim" not only the best students, but also the most flexible, innovative teachers. In fact, some magnets have been carefully designed to attract the most gifted and talented students to a program designed to challenge them to learn to their potential. These programs provide advantages that offset any disadvantages, which may include the lack of a diverse curriculum and extracurricular activities.

One answer to this concern is to create more magnet schools and to encourage all students to participate in the unique educational opportunities associated with school choice. In addition, many urban school districts use quotas to ensure that magnet schools attract a diverse group of students that reflects the diversity in the surrounding community.

Are magnet schools really any different? Yet another challenge confronting magnet schools is that so many of them were created in the midst of court-ordered desegregation with little or no time to train staff, inform parents, and develop appropriate curricula. As a result, many "special theme" magnets simply failed to live up to their promise of unique curricular programs. A 1974–75 external evaluation of the more than 20 alternative schools in Berkeley, California, uncovered a marked similarity in all of the available educational options there. The evaluators concluded that the alternative schools lacked sufficient distinctiveness to permit a rational choice among them. Similarly, a review of the early Boston magnet schools reported that "after two years, most of the magnet school principals . . . admit privately that their magnet theme is grossly underdeveloped—or non-existent" (Barr, 1982, p. 40).

Despite these early problems, a second and third generation of students who are attending magnet schools are finding that these innovative educational opportunities are significantly, often dramatically, different from traditional schools. This is especially true in the career-theme magnet schools.

Should magnet schools strive to be better than other schools? Too often, magnets appear to have been built on the assumption that they provide better, higher-quality education than do other schools in the district. But such an assumption often poses a difficult problem. Magnet schools must strive for a distinctiveness that is best for certain students, just as other options, including the conventional school program, are best for others. For the magnet school to be successful, the choice must not be between high-quality schools and mediocre ones. Rational choice demands distinctive curricula, teaching styles, and career opportunities that provide equal access for *all* youth. However, it is true that many magnet schools academically outperform other public and private schools (Raywid, 1990).

How should a district help parents choose? One of the most important challenges facing magnet schools is helping parents, students, and teachers gain sufficient, reliable information to make an appropriate decision for their child's education.

Most school districts that offer a large number of magnets provide information and discussion sessions, videotapes that demonstrate what the school offers, public service announcements, mailed information booklets and brochures, and community forums and meetings. Marketing approaches also must reflect the multicultural dimension of the community, which often requires multilingual promotion of the available choices. Information and help sessions in neighborhoods during the application period also can dramatically increase interest and participation.

Can a district change traditional schools into magnet schools? One of the challenges for school districts is to make the transition from conventional schools to a diversified system of neighborhood schools and magnet programs. The best option has been to create new, smaller magnet schools in cooperation with business, industry, and community agencies and to house the new magnets in off-campus sites. Another approach that has worked well is to create schools within schools. These dual-program schools serve as both a local neighborhood and a districtwide magnet opportunity. However, if the development of magnets demands that new facilities be built or leased, local taxpayers may object.

The Cincinnati Public Schools, striving to increase districtwide magnet offerings, recently mandated that all non-magnet schools participate in an accepted model of schoolwide change. In Texas, schools have approached this change in a very harsh manner; in San Antonio, Corpus Christi, and other cities, school districts have "deinstitutionalized" one or more local schools so that all of the teachers, administrators, and students must be reassigned to a new school. This frees up the "deinstitutionalized" building to house a new magnet school. Such an approach creates anxieties, frustrations, and anger and should be avoided if at all possible.

Another approach, used in New York's Central Park East, is to house several magnet programs in a single building. At Central Park East, a single school building houses five separate programs, each with its own director and without a building principal.

TRANSPORTATION: A VEXING CHALLENGE

When we first started our districtwide magnet school program, we could have used Dwight Eisenhower and the skills he used to coordinate air, sea, and land forces in the D-Day invasion of Europe. We could find no other school district in the country that had ever tried such a complicated transportation system to ensure parents that they could get their kids to the school of their choice. I'll never forget that first day when kids all over town left their neighborhoods and attendance areas to be bused all over town to the new magnet schools. Our greatest fear was that at the end of the first day, parents all over town would be calling to find out why their kids didn't come home. We just pounded it into our bus drivers, "For God's sake, drive safely and don't lose any kids."

Midwestern School Administrator

The one aspect of magnet schools that almost destroyed the concept before it could be tried was transportation. It was hard enough for school districts to confine transportation systems to carefully prescribed attendance zones; to get students to new magnet schools located all over town proved to be all but impossible. In many communities, it was the threat of court-ordered compulsory busing that prompted the first experiments. But as districts across the country began developing multiple magnet schools and permitting parents and students to volunteer for these programs, they worked hard to develop transportation systems that were able to meet the challenge.

Today the most frequently used approach involves transportation cycles. First, students are picked up in their local neighborhood and carried to "staging areas," where they transfer to another bus—to be transported to their magnet school.

Some school districts are unable to provide all children with bus transportation. In Los Angeles, parents apply for a P.F.T.—a Permit for Transportation—and a particular magnet program (or their top three choices). If they do not receive a P.F.T., parents must use city bus services or drive their children to the schools of choice.

In Chicago, elementary students are provided transportation to the school of their choice at no cost if they live at least 1½ miles from the school. Transportation is not provided for high school students. Chicago also offers this disclaimer to parents: "It may not be possible for your child to be enrolled in certain schools because it is not feasible to establish a transportation route for one or very few students."

RESEARCH ON MAGNET SCHOOLS

Because of the large number of magnet schools, their urban location, and their relationship to racial integration, magnet schools have been studied carefully over the course of their development. The results support the effectiveness of these schools yet do identify concerns.

Magnet schools have been found to contribute to effective desegregation programs. A study by ABT Associates (1978) of magnet schools in 18 districts concluded that "only a limited amount of desegregation can be attributed to magnet schools. However, magnet schools can be an effective desegregation device when used as a component of a comprehensive, district-wide desegregation effort" (p. 11).

Yet a growing body of information attests to the effectiveness of magnet schools in other areas. Some data indicate that there is a surprising reduction in violence and vandalism in magnet schools—even those specifically designed to attract delinquent or disruptive youth. In this age of heightened violence in communities and schools, to find that magnet schools are safe havens for learning is usually enough to create huge waiting lists of anxious parents in violent neighborhoods trying to enroll their children in a violence-free school.

When compared to regular public schools, most magnet schools report better attendance rates and significant increases in the numbers of students participating in extracurricular activities. Improved student self-concept and better attitudes toward school are also among the benefits cited in the research. In 1977, the Educational Research Service synthesized evaluation data from more than 25 alternative and magnet schools representing a wide variety of programs. Their report concluded, "In most cases, the academic achievement of students improved or remained stable" (Doob, 1977, p. 44).

Recent research has found even more promising achievement gains. As magnet schools have matured and have developed highly distinctive programs focusing on careers and professions, student achievement has continued to improve. In the most recent study, magnet school students were found to have higher achievement than students in either comprehensive public schools or parochial schools (Gamoran, 1996a).

Two major school evaluation projects in the 1980s, one in Los Angeles and the other in New York state, have verified the positive impact of magnet schools. In Los Angeles, virtually all of the magnet programs' students scored at or above district and national levels on tests of reading and mathematics achievement. The longer students had been in a magnet, the greater their relative achievement and the more positive their attitude toward school. Magnet school students at all levels in Los Angeles feel more positive about school than do other students in the district (Estes, Levine, & Walter, 1990).

External evaluators in New York reported similar findings. The investigators concluded that magnet schools help students arrive at higher achievement levels in reading and mathematics, both at elementary and secondary levels, and for both minority and majority students. Almost all the parents (98% of those responding to a survey) and teachers reported "high satisfaction" with the magnet schools with which they were associated. The evaluators also reported a new finding: "The establishment of schools of choice is a powerful stimulus to improve all of our district schools" (Estes, Levine, & Walter, 1990, p. 43).

In spite of these positive findings, at least two major concerns have been identified. One large national study found that more than half of all secondary magnet schools and approximately a quarter of elementary magnet schools utilized some type of admission testing. Since the specialized curricula of magnets are designed to attract particular types of students, many magnets use admission tests to help identify and select the students they seek. Few other conventional or alternative public schools use admission tests, and charter schools are expressly denied the use of any testing or screening mechanisms. Selective admissions can limit equal opportunity.

A second concern regarding magnet schools is that many of them spend more per pupil than other schools in their districts. A 1986–87 study in St. Louis found that the school district was spending 42% more per pupil in magnet schools than in other district schools. In particular, magnet high schools spent 27% more per pupil than other comprehensive high schools.

Similar findings have been reported in Boston, Chicago, New York, and Philadelphia (Nathan, 1996).

TWO MODEL SCHOOL DISTRICTS

The Jefferson County Public Schools in Louisville, Kentucky, and the Houston Independent School District in Houston, Texas, can serve as examples of how a comprehensive approach to magnet schools can truly diversify a district. These districts have made the implementation and expansion of magnet programs a priority. Today they serve as models for districts throughout the nation.

JEFFERSON COUNTY SCHOOL DISTRICT

The Jefferson County School District (JCSD) is a recognized leader in school restructuring and educational reform. As one of the country's 25 largest school districts, JCSD serves 97,000 students (infants through adults) at 150 locations. In 1972, the district created its first alternative school, the Brown School. Located originally in the former Brown Hotel, the school served diverse students (by quotas) in grades 3 to 12 in a self-directed, open education environment. Today the K–12 Brown School is located in a former downtown office building and is a member of the Coalition of Essential Schools.

JCSD offers dozens of choices at the elementary, middle, and high school levels. Each year, more than 9,000 students apply for positions in the district's 87 alternative schools and programs. In an effort to achieve an appropriate mix of students at each site, a common set of criteria for selection of students includes consideration of race, gender, and geographic location based on postal ZIP codes. Some alternatives have additional and unique selection criteria, including talent screenings for the performing arts programs. The Louisville public schools emphasize that all students have choices, though they are managed choices to ensure an appropriate mix of students and the availability of transportation. The Jefferson County School District (1995) offers the following educational options at the various grade levels.

EARLY CHILDHOOD EDUCATION/ALTERNATIVES

- Byck Elementary Cradle School: This school helps parents prepare students for school.

- Jump Start: This half-day preschool for three-year-olds helps to enrich learning for young children.

- Child Care Enrichment: This before- and after-school program for young children is conducted in partnership with the YMCA and focuses on learning and enrichment.

- Other programs at the early childhood level: Head Start, Pre-Kindergarten, and Preschool

ELEMENTARY SCHOOLS AND ALTERNATIVES

- Home School: The home school is the school that serves the student's address.

- Cluster: Each home school is a member of a school cluster consisting of five to seven schools per cluster. Parent choices—made on the basis of a variety of programs offered at each school within the cluster—are granted based on building capacity and racial-balance guidelines. Transportation is provided within the cluster.

- Magnet Schools: Seven elementary magnet schools include those with a focus on traditional programs; mathematics, science, and technology; self-directed learning; and Montessori.

- Magnet Programs: Located within five conventional schools, these include programs with a focus on traditional programs; gifted and talented; science, technology, and environmental education; and international studies and foreign language.

MIDDLE SCHOOLS AND ALTERNATIVES

- Interdisciplinary Teaming: All of the district's middle schools use a team approach to instruction. Teams of three to six teachers share the same students, the same part of the school building, and the same planning time. Teaming, which is like a school within a school, allows teachers to get to know students and their academic and emotional needs.

- Home School: The home school is the school that serves the student's address.

- Magnet Schools: These include four schools that focus on traditional programs and self-directed learning. School assignments are based on the student's address.

- Magnet Programs: These four programs focus on international studies; mathematics, science, and technology; and gifted and talented.

- Optional Programs: An option is a small, specialized program in a particular school. Optional programs are developed by local school staffs for their students. Seven optional programs include environmental and life science, liberal arts, traditional, visual and performing arts, career technologies, communications, and humanities/ fine arts.

HIGH SCHOOLS AND ALTERNATIVES

- Home School: The home school is the school that serves the student's address.

- Magnet Schools: These include six schools that focus on self-directed learning; traditional programs with an engineering focus; communications and media arts; mathematics, science, and technology; the visual arts; and acting, dance, instrumental music, piano, theater, and vocal music.

- Magnet Programs and Magnet Career Academies: Four-year academic and technical magnet programs are offered within comprehensive high school settings. These 12 programs include medicine and allied health; business management, entrepreneurship, banking, finance, and accounting; computer technology; legal/governmental services; childcare services; pre-engineering; cosmetology; public safety technology, including law enforcement, fire science, and emergency medical technology; electronic communications; health/fitness careers; building technologies; chemical plastics technologies; horticulture and urban agriscience; future educators; aviation technology; and many others.

- Optional Programs: An option is a small, specialized program in a particular school. Four optional programs have been developed by local school staffs for their students.

- Open Enrollment: The district's open-enrollment policy gives incoming ninth-grade students the opportunity to choose the high school they want to attend.

HOUSTON INDEPENDENT SCHOOL DISTRICT

The Houston Independent School District, which serves a student population in excess of 200,000, is administratively subdivided into 12 semi-autonomous districts. Eleven of those districts are contiguous geographic areas, and one of the districts is comprised of the various alternative schools and programs from around the school district (Houston Independent School District, 1996).

The Alternative District schools are grouped into clusters by type of programs offered, common characteristics and demographics, and other factors:

- Cluster A schools are magnet schools at which students apply for admission and are chosen on a competitive basis. The screening involved is specific to the focus of the individual school.

- Cluster B schools are designed for students who are at high risk for dropping out of school. These schools vary in their focus and types of students served. They range from a school for seriously emotionally disturbed students to a high school for academically capable students who have fallen seriously behind in their coursework.

- Cluster C schools are designed for adjudicated youth, located in the detention facilities to which the students have been assigned.

- Cluster D schools are collaborative education programs owned and operated by agencies not affiliated with the public school system. With one exception, these schools prepare students for the General Educational Development (GED) examination, rather than offer high school diplomas. The Houston Independent School District has contractual agreements with these organizations to provide technical support and a portion of the state revenue generated by the students enrolled in their programs.

HOUSTON ALTERNATIVE SCHOOL PROGRAMS

- Community Services programs address the needs of students who are confined to their homes, hospitals, or agency sites as a result of physical, mental, or emotional disabilities. Both regular and special education services are available through age 21.

- Kay Ongoing Education Center and Crittenton Center are alternative schools that serve pregnant students in grades 6–12. In addition to teaching all the required subjects, the centers provide comprehensive health care and a special curriculum for becoming a good parent.

- Crossroads is an intervention program for students in grades 7–12 who are chemically dependent. The voluntary six-week program is open to nonviolent students who would otherwise be suspended or expelled for violations of the Code of Student Conduct.

- Contemporary Learning Center features continuous-progress instruction for secondary students who are at risk of dropping out, who have not been successful in the traditional classroom, and who are not achieving their potential.

- Terrell Alternative Middle School offers a comprehensive academic and developmental program for at-risk youngsters who have been referred by their home schools to an alternative setting because of aggressive or antisocial behavior.

- Harper Alternative School serves students with disabilities, ages 15–22, who require vocational training; at-risk exceptional students, ages 12–22, diagnosed as having severe emotional disturbances; and students who have violated the Code of Student Conduct by bringing weapons to school and who have received probation from juvenile court.

- Foley's Academy, developed in cooperation with Foley's Department Store and Houston Communities in Schools, targets academically capable underachievers. Individualized, self-paced instruction features flexible scheduling and is geared to college-bound youngsters.

- Carter Career Center offers a career-oriented program that motivates at-risk students and dropouts to come to school, stay in school, graduate or earn a General Educational Development (GED) certificate, and enter the workforce.

- George I. Sanchez High School began as a privately funded, community-based alternative school for young people who have dropped out of public schools for one semester or more.

- Harris County Juvenile Detention Center, a secure temporary residential facility, serves youths who have been detained by Harris County law enforcement officers and are awaiting court action.

- Harris County Youth Village and Burnett-Bayland Home are minimum-security court-placement residential facilities for adjudicated youths, ages 11–17, operated by the Harris County Juvenile Probation Department.

- High School for Health Professions offers a comprehensive pre-college program that prepares students for careers in medicine, health care, and the sciences. Instruction features access to the Texas Medical Center and other health and research facilities throughout the city.

- High School for Law Enforcement and Criminal Justice combines strong academic courses with in-depth study of the criminal justice system. Law-related vocational courses cover everything from fingerprinting and pre-sentence hearings to legal contracts and search and seizure. At graduation, students are prepared to enter law enforcement and other law-related careers.

- High School for the Performing and Visual Arts is the first school in the Southwest to combine an outstanding academic program with intensive, highly specialized professional training for students who are talented in instrumental or vocal music, theater, dance, and the visual arts.

- Barbara Jordan High School for Careers is a vocational magnet school that teaches students the skills they need for the job market along with the academic subjects they need to earn their high school diplomas. Jordan also offers STRIVE (Stepping Toward Renewal in Vocational Education), a program for over-age, low-performing ninth graders at risk of dropping out; Vocational Education for the Handicapped, for students with disabilities that limit their performance in a regular classroom; and the Regional Day School for the Deaf, for students whose hearing impairment has had an adverse effect on academic performance in a traditional classroom.

- Houston Night High School, which uses the facilities of Milby High School, offers instruction during the evening for at-risk students, ages 15–21, who cannot attend school during regular daytime hours because of employment or obligations as parents.

- Langston Family Life Center is a partnership formed by HISD, the United Way of the Texas Gulf Coast, and the Texas Department of Human Services that offers a full range of community services.

  - The Career Center features career investigation classes for eighth-grade students and vocational testing and job placement services for high school students.

♦ Target Hunger is a model food pantry that supplies food and services to residents of the nearby neighborhoods.

♦ The Early Childhood Development Center has half-day (morning and afternoon) pre-kindergarten for three- and four-year-olds who are not yet proficient in English or who qualify for free or reduced-price lunch. Full-day kindergarten is available for children who turn five years old no later than September 1.

♦ The Success by Six program focuses on children's readiness for school from the prenatal stage to age six by offering education and case management for parents.

♦ GED classes are held on site, primarily for Job Opportunity Basic Skills (JOBS) participants who reside in the zip codes surrounding Langston.

♦ The Life Skills class meets in two-week cycles, Monday through Friday, for JOBS participants who reside in the surrounding zip codes.

♦ The Eligibility Program helps low-income families meet basic needs with food stamps, Aid to Families with Dependent Children (AFDC) and Women and Infant Care (WIC) certification and distribution, health screening, and immunizations. This office accepts and screens application forms.

CONCLUSION

Magnet schools are standard operating procedure in many districts. While originally started to counter the ill effects of segregation, today magnet schools enjoy substantial support from the business community, parents, and children. Magnets provide focus, choice, and real-world learning opportunities and applications.

Magnets often offer a family a chance to substantially increase their participation and commitment to public education. Every effective magnet school represents yet another alternative school for parents and children. In the foreseeable future, many believe that all levels of public education will offer these effective programs and schools.

REFERENCES

ABT Associates. (1978). *Final report: Study of the Elementary School Aid Act for magnet school programs.* Washington, DC: U.S. Office of Education.

Barr, R.D. (1982, January). Magnet schools: An attractive alternative. *Principal,* 37–40.

Doob, H.S. (1977). *Evaluation of alternative schools.* Arlington, VA: Educational Research Service.

Estes, N., Levine, D.U., & Walter, W.R. (Eds.). (1990). *Magnet schools: Recent developments and perspectives.* Austin, TX: Morgan Printing and Publishing.

Gamoran, R.A. (1996a, Spring). Student achievement in public magnet, public comprehensive, and private city high schools. *Educational Evaluation and Policy Analysis, 18,* 1–18.

Gamoran, R.A. (1996b, October). Do magnet schools boost achievement? *Educational Leadership, 54.*

Houston Independent School District. (1996). *Alternative schools: Unique opportunities for academic success.* Houston: Author.

Jefferson County Public Schools. (1995). *A guide to optional programs and magnet schools for elementary, middle, and high school students.* Louisville, KY: Author.

Magnet Schools of America. (1996). *Directory of public magnet and theme-based schools.* Houston: Author.

McMillan, C.B. (1977, November). Magnet education in Boston. *Phi Delta Kappan, 59,* 158–163.

McMillan, C.B. (1980). *Magnet schools: An approach to voluntary desegregation* (Fastback 141). Bloomington, IN: Phi Delta Kappa Educational Foundation.

Nathan, J. (1996). *Charter schools: Creating hope and opportunity for American education.* San Francisco: Jossey-Bass.

Raywid, M.A. (1990). The accomplishments of schools of choice. In N. Estes, D.U. Levine, & W.R. Walter (Eds.), *Magnet schools: Recent developments and perspectives.* Austin, TX: Morgan Printing and Publishing.

Strickland, C. (1996). The rainbow connection: Portrait of a microsociety, magnet school in action. *New Schools, New Communities, 12* (3), 60–65.

Students learn more in magnets than other schools, study finds. (1996, March 4). *Education Week,* p. 21.

Charter Schools

During my second term, my goal is to have 3,000 new charter schools in operation in America.

President Bill Clinton

Wait a minute, wait a minute! Do you mean to tell me that we can actually "own" our public school? Can that be possible?

Teacher,
Michigan

Well, our charter school is housed in this pitiful, dilapidated and dusty old storefront building. We are working seven days a week and twelve hours a day; but we can't blame the principal if something goes wrong, because we don't have one. Like the employees of United Airlines, we own this enterprise! This is our school! So we are all working harder than any of us have ever worked, but we are only limited by our own energy and creativity. For long-term public school teachers, we are just in "hog heaven." This is as close to "ideal" as teaching could ever possibly get.

Charter School Teacher,
California

I N FOUR YEARS, CHARTERS HAVE GONE from a little-noticed idea in Minnesota, a state that always seems willing to experiment with public education, to a national movement involving half of the states and growing funding from the federal government. And the concept is gaining momentum. By the summer of 1996, more than 350 charter schools, serving about 28,000 students, were in operation in the United States. By mid-fall about 500 charters were in operation serving over 100,000 students. During the 1996 presidential election, charter schools were championed by the Democratic Party as an alternative to education vouchers, which were supported by the Republican Party. As a result, the visibility of charter schools increased and even became an issue in the presidential debates.

Charter school legislation usually allows groups of teachers, parents, and some private individuals or agencies to apply to be chartered to operate schools that are publicly funded but are free of many regulations, and often free even of teacher contracts. Many charter school proponents believe that it is the excessive rules and regulations that paralyze creative approaches to teaching, learning, and school finance.

Charter schools can be considered part of the deregulation movement. Just as deregulation dramatically transformed the savings and loan industry, the communications industry, and the airline industry, a growing number of states (for example, Texas, Michigan, South Dakota, and California) have significantly revised and reduced the number of regulations governing public education. Twenty-five states have passed legislation that permits "charter" public schools to be developed, funded, and operated with a minimum of state and local regulation.

However, reducing the number of state regulations that govern public education has not led to complete deregulation. Public school charters continue to be scrutinized, controlled, limited, and litigated. The struggle to establish charter schools has demonstrated the power of teachers' unions and the education establishment and how resistant they can be to change.

Charter schools have been at the center of vicious political and legal debates regarding issues of money and control. For reform-minded public educators who have toiled during the past 25 years in alternative schools, charter school legislation is often an answer to their prayers. For school boards, superintendents, and teachers' unions, charter schools often are perceived as a major problem.

Albert Shanker has focused the power and influence of the American Federation of Teachers (AFT) on charter schools to, as he says, "refine the concept." Yet, both the AFT and the NEA insist on controlling charter school development which has become the focus of continuing, heated controversy. Some school boards and local teachers' unions, especially in several large urban school districts, have made charter schools difficult if not impossible to initiate. Because of this, the majority of new charter schools in the United States have been opened in smaller cities and in suburban and rural districts. To date, approximately 20% of the charter schools currently in operation are former alternative schools that have chosen to convert.

While 25 states have passed charter school legislation, the concept has been defeated in a number of other states, most recently in Washington state. Even in many of the states that have passed charter school legislation, a variety of conditions have been imposed that significantly limit the number of charter schools and restrain their freedom.

WHAT IS A CHARTER SCHOOL?

To create a charter school, state legislatures first must pass enabling legislation. Where this new policy has been established, it permits school districts or states to transfer responsibility for public education to groups of teachers, parents, or interested individuals. With the exception of a few First Amendment guarantees, charter school legislation allows for most state and local regulations that govern public education to be relaxed or waived. In return, the state requires accountability standards that mandate the documentation of student achievement for the school. Thus charter schools gain the freedom to redesign or reinvent public education.

For many years, school districts have contracted with private firms to provide such services as bus transportation and food, and occasionally private firms provided entire academic programs, usually focused on at-risk or incarcerated youth. And in a few cases, public districts have privatized schools or entire districts by contracting with private entrepreneurs or a college or university.

Charter schools take this "contract" concept a dramatic step further. For the first time in the United States, more than one group in a community has the opportunity to organize and operate a public school. Teachers, business people, nonprofit organizations, parents, public agency personnel, and a host of others can form a cooperative or a partnership and essentially become educational entrepreneurs. These groups then enter into a contract, or charter, to run their own school. According to the specific legislation in each state, these charters can be authorized by local school districts, state boards of education, a college or university, or some combination of authorizing agencies.

The following description of the Georgia charter school legislation explains the concept:

> *In effect, charter schools will be self-regulated like a chartered business. The "charter" will be a binding performance contract between the charter school, its local board of education and the State Board of Education. This charter, when approved by the local board of education and the State Board of Education, will substitute for state education statutes as well as state and local rules, policies, regulations and standards as a governance structure for the charter school. With the freedom provided under the Charter Schools Act, schools will be able to rethink and redesign "from the ground up," including, but not limited to, what students learn, how it is packaged and how it is delivered; how school instructional staff are deployed, how students are placed, grouped and scheduled; how school decisions are made; how funds are allocated and used; and how the community is involved in supporting the school; as well as defining the rules, roles, and responsibilities of all involved in schooling* (Wilt, 1993, p. 10).

CHARACTERISTICS OF CHARTER SCHOOLS

Not all charter school legislation is created equal. In fact, there is a tremendous variation in the 25 states that have passed charter legislation. Many critics feel that only half of the states provide for "true" charter schools that are clearly "outside the box"; the rest of the states, they argue, have diluted the idea. Some of these diluted laws continue to give local school districts controlling authority over charter schools. Some charter legislation seems to be little more than "site-based management." Some states go further by making local school boards the only entity to authorize charters, which all but dictates the terms of the charter and ensures continuing local control. A recent analysis, funded by the Pew Charitable Trusts, provides a careful evaluation of the various charter school legislations. This analysis clearly indicates that state legislation which requires charter school authorization to be controlled by local or state school boards has a limiting effect on the development of new schools. (See Figure 1 on p. 141.)

However, there are a number of elements that have come to define charter schools.

First, a charter school is a public school. Charters must be nonsectarian, may not charge tuition, and cannot use admission tests or any other device to screen student applications. They must take all who apply as long as there is room in the school. And, like all other public schools, they must follow constitutional guarantees and health and safety regulations. However, once a charter school is established, it becomes almost completely autonomous; thus it is like a one-school district.

Because they are legal entities, charters provide for comprehensive site-based management and the creation of local governing boards. Teachers usually can choose to join the local bargaining unit, form their own bargaining unit, or decide that, as owners, they no longer need a bargaining unit.

Charter schools also are schools of choice. Charter school legislation permits no admission tests (with the exception of certain types of schools, such as schools for the performing arts, which can hold auditions) and requires that families, students, and teachers choose to participate. The element of choice in public education likely accounts for a large portion of the success of charter schools.

In order to stay open, charter schools must achieve the student performance objectives that are agreed to in the charter and must continue to attract sufficient numbers of parents and

FIGURE 1

	STRONGER									WEAKER					
AZ ('94)	MI ('94)	DE ('95)	NH ('95)	MS ('93)	TX ('95)	CA ('92)	MN ('91)	CO ('93)	LA ('95)	WI ('93)	HA ('94)	WY ('95)	NM ('93)	RI ('95)	GA ('93)	KS ('94)	AR ('95)	AK ('95)

ARIZONA

No law perfectly embodies the charter concept, but Arizona's comes closest. Lawmakers revised the law this year.

Cap: None. **Schools open:** 47.*

Approval: Any public body, private person, or private organization may organize a school. Either a local school board, the state board of education, or the state board for charter schools can sponsor a charter.

State/local control: All charter schools are automatically exempt from state laws except those regarding health, safety, civil rights, insurance, and children with disabilities or special needs. Local districts have no legal authority over schools sponsored by the state board of education or the state board for charter schools.

Private school eligibility: Yes, if the school is nonsectarian, but it must become a public school and no longer accept tuition.

Hiring: Schools are not required to hire certified teachers.

MINNESOTA

The state that pioneered the charter concept revisited its law to strengthen it in 1993 and 1995.

Cap: Increased to 40 schools this year after it was originally set at eight and, later, 12 schools. **Schools open:** 17.*

Approval: Only licensed teachers can operate a school, and the school's charter must first be approved by a local school board, community college, state university, or technical college. The state board of education must give final approval. Such an approval process is more limiting than Arizona's, but in 1993, lawmakers amended the original law so that charter applicants rejected by the local school board can appeal to the state board if two members of the local school board voted to approve their charter.

State/local control: Schools are automatically exempt from state laws and local district policies except those regarding health, safety, civil rights, and children with disabilities or special needs. The schools have complete control of the money they receive from the state.

Private school eligibility: Yes, if the school is nonsectarian, but it must become a public school and no longer accept tuition.

Hiring: Schools can hire only certified teachers.

GEORGIA

Charter advocates say the Georgia law encourages site-based management of schools but has little to do with the charter concept. It is one of the toughest states in which to start a school.

Cap: None. **Schools open:** 3.*

Approval: Schools can only be organized by Georgia public school staff or faculty. For an existing public school to become a charter school, two-thirds of the faculty and staff must agree. Schools must be approved by the local school board and the state board of education.

State/local control: All schools remain under the authority of the local school board.

Private school eligibility: No.

Hiring: Schools can hire noncertified teachers if they get a waiver from the district and state.

Reprinted with permission from *Education Week*, Special Report, "Breaking Away: Charter School Revolution," November 29, 1995.

*As of February, 1977, there were 113 charter schools in operation in Arizona, 19 in Minnesota, and 12 in Georgia.

students to maintain established enrollment levels. Some states require charter school students to comply with statewide testing policy to determine student achievement.

In California, charters for new schools must contain:

> . . . *a description of student outcomes which are clearly stated, that reflect student engagement in a rich and challenging curriculum, and which are measurable. All charter schools will be required to administer the new statewide assessments and to meet the performance standards which are developed in conjunction with these standards. In addition to these required assessments, charter school petitioners and local governing boards should agree on a comprehensive set of measures which will, together with the required statewide tests, give both the school and the district a clear picture of how the school and its students are doing* (Wilt, 1993, p. 11).

Another common characteristic of charter schools is the waiver of many state and local education regulations. With the exception of health, safety, and fire codes and, in some locations, earthquake building codes, almost all of the rules and regulations—in some states, even union contracts—are waived for charter schools. The amount of regulations actually waived differs from state to state. For example, many states do not require charter schools to hire only certified teachers. However, other states require that none but certified teachers or administrators can serve as instructional personnel.

In exchange for the waiver of educational regulations, the charter school agrees to provide solid evidence of student achievement.

Because they are public schools, charter schools receive state and local funds. Charter school funding usually is based on the per-pupil costs in the local school district. Most states specify some percentage of the regular per-pupil cost. In Colorado, for example, charter schools receive 80% of the per-pupil cost of the local school district. The remaining funds stay with the local district to pay for those services that the district provides, such as transportation, purchasing, personnel, payroll, etc. (Wilt, 1993).

Charter schools usually receive these funds without the line-item restrictions that normally are placed on funds for public schools. This allows the charter school's funds to be used in the most flexible, creative, and useful manner. For example, charter schools can choose not to hire administrators and, instead, use these savings to hire increased numbers of paraprofessionals or to purchase educational technology.

> *Imagine a school district modeled not on the practices of General Motors but on those of a cottage industry. The average per-pupil expenditure in this country is about $5,260 a year. Envision a small, highly autonomous school, given that funding level. If the school has 200 kids in it, its annual operating budget is over $1,050,000. Return 20 percent of it—$210,000—to a trimmed-down central administration for its reduced services and for bus transportation. Imagine a low student/teacher ration, say 20:1. Pay your 10 teachers well, say an average of $45,000 a year (including fringe benefits). Hire a head teacher and pay him or her $60,000. Find an appropriate building for your program in your community and rent it at $7,000 a month plus another $3,000 for utilities. Hire a secretary, a custodian, and a cleaning person at $20,000 each. Budget $1,000 a year for supplies for each of your teachers and $3,000 for the central office. Put aside $10,000 to buy books each year and*

*$20,000 for computers and A-V equipment. If the idea of trips is appealing, lease three vans, each at $5,000 dollars a year. That's probably enough to cover maintenance of them, but include another $3,000 just to be sure. Put $12,000 into a mileage budget. Now comes the fun: figuring out what to do with the $70,000 that has yet to be spent (Gregory, 1993, p. 224).**

Charter schools also place teachers in new roles. Teachers become planners, managers, small-business owners, and coordinators of learning. In addition to the traditional responsibilities of instruction, each professional teacher often supervises and coordinates a number of instructional aides and other paraprofessionals who assist in some aspect of student instruction. Techniques of shared decision making, coupled with small school size and a staff that chooses to participate, reduce the need to invest in multiple school administrators. Parents and volunteers also can help staff with the tasks of administering the school.

Teachers who participate in a charter school usually are protected in some way. For example, teachers usually are allowed to take a leave of absence from their school in order to work in a charter school and thus retain seniority while on leave. They also are permitted to continue to participate in the local and state retirement programs. In addition, charter school faculty often are permitted to maintain active participation in the local union or to create their own professional organization through which they collectively own and operate the school.

Charter schools often make extensive use of paraprofessionals. (See Figure 2 on p. 145.) In addition, they usually use many volunteers and part-time teachers from business, industry, the arts, and nearby colleges and universities to supplement the curriculum, mentor students, and provide tutorial services.

FIGURE 2

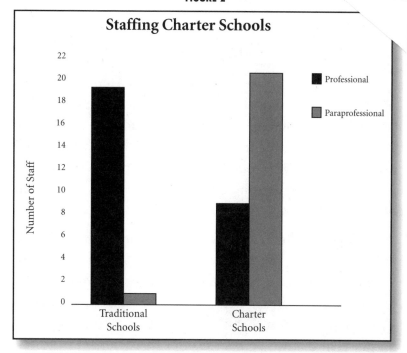

Staffing Charter Schools

WHY CHARTER SCHOOLS?

In a recent survey by the Center for School Change (1996) in Minneapolis, 62 legislators in seven states were asked about the reasons for introducing charter legislation. The researchers found five primary purposes:

- Help students who have not succeeded in existing schools.

- Provide opportunities for educational entrepreneurs.

- Expand the range of schools available.

- Increase student achievement.

- Encourage the existing system to change.

Pressure on states to consider charter schools has occurred for a number of other reasons, including complaints about the inertia of large education bureaucracies and the stifling regulations that restrict education reform. Charter schools are often seen as a very cost-effective way to reform the schools. Indeed, they are instituting major reforms within the existing per-pupil costs.

Charter schools also have received support from a variety of groups for political reasons. For example, in California the growth of interest in some type of statewide voucher plan tended to consolidate support for the less controversial charter legislation. Out of fear that California citizens would approve a voucher plan that would have tax dollars channeled to private schools, a diverse group of professional and private groups emerged to support the charter legislation (Wilt, 1993).

However, the driving force behind charter schools has been the desire to improve education for all students. Charter legislation has been supported by school boards, businesses, and by innovative and alternative school educators who see the concept as a way of gaining freedom from regulation and gaining ownership of their local school. Colorado Governor Roy Romer explained that a charter school is:

> *The opportunity to completely rethink and redesign a public school—from its overall vision for students, to its educational program, to the relationship between the school and its teachers, to assessment, to administrative practices and governance. It requires that a charter school, as a public school, meet public impera-*

tives of accountability and equity, but does not require that it be all things to all people. Charter school activity has the potential to create a more vibrant and diverse range of public school programs available for parents and students who want and need alternatives to the conventional approach (Romer, 1993, p. 1).

CHARTER SCHOOL PROBLEMS AND CONTROVERSY

Many in public education see charter schools as the final battleground. Having struggled with home schooling, vouchers, schools of choice, privatization, alternative routes to teacher certification, employee union contracts, and even alternative schools, many local school boards have drawn a "line in the sand" and have joined with teacher unions and a variety of others in a counterattack on charters. Several key concerns regarding charter schools have been identified by the American Federation of Teachers and focus on the issues of money, power, and teacher certification. They include:

- Loss of adequate control for existing school boards and local school districts.

- Seventeen states do not require the use of certified teachers.

- Lack of adequate objective measures to assess student achievement in charter schools.

- Lack of requirements to compare charter school students with other public school students.

- While all 25 states prohibit charter schools from charging tuition, many still allow them to charge "fees" and solicit "donations," practices that resemble proxies for tuition.

- Most states do not require charter schools to be approved by the local host school district ("Charter school resources," 1995).

Legislation in a number of states permits schools to be chartered by the state superintendent or state board of education, another state agency, or even a college or university. Thus many fear that there are no adequate controls or safeguards for the local "host" school district. In addition, most critics of charter schools maintain that there are not sufficient objective measurements to adequately document student achievement in charter schools. Further, they assert that there are insufficient requirements in the country with which to assess charter school students' achievement and to compare results to other public school students.

One particular concern focuses on the mismanagement of the charter concept by unscrupulous individuals or by people who have tried to use charter schools for ulterior motives. In California, one charter school, Edutrain, went bankrupt with more than a million dollars unaccounted for. The principal of the school appeared to have used public funds to pay his rent, hire a bodyguard, and fund a $7,000 staff retreat on the Pacific coast. Another charter school in Michigan was challenged in court for being little more than an electronic network for home schoolers (Molnar, 1996). Overall, few charter schools have been closed; yet there continue to be court challenges and criticism in this area.

Directly related to concerns regarding mismanagement is the fact that most educators lack business and budget experience. While the idea of an employee-owned business is attractive to many public school teachers, charter school proprietors often discover that they lack sufficient "expertise or the resources to monitor and enforce [their] charters" (Molnar, 1996). Few public school teachers or parents have had any experience with budgets of the size and complexity to operate a school. Charter school proprietors often lack the business managers, accountants, and legal advice that every school district in the country routinely employs. And like all new small businesses, the possibility of failure remains high. Skeptics predict that there soon will be a rash of news stories about educational mismanagement in charter schools.

A major problem that has confronted charter schools is the lack of start-up funds. Few of the state legislatures have provided funds in the various charter school authorizations for planning, development, teacher training, equipment, instructional materials, and facilities. As a result, most charter schools are faced with enormous problems in getting their schools opened for business. Nearly all are forced to seek grants and donations and to sponsor fund-raising activities. Inadequate financial support and the lack of start-up funds are the most frequently mentioned problems by charter school owners (Education Commission of the States and Center for School Change, 1995).

Directly related to the volatile issues of power and control, teacher certification and union contracts almost always become issues of conflict. Most charters use a wide variety of individuals with special talents, such as an astronomer, a political scientist, or a professional artist. While nearly all charter schools use some certified teachers, the role of the certified teacher often is changed dramatically to that of a planner, supervisor, and coordinator of teaching and learning. Seventeen states do not require the use of certified teachers, an issue of grave concern for teachers' unions.

In spite of the harsh criticism of charters by the National Education Association (NEA) and the American Federation of Teachers (AFT), both organizations indicate they are willing to become involved in the creation of charter schools. The NEA recently has announced a million-dollar program to work with state affiliates to start charters in Arizona, California, Colorado, Georgia, Hawaii, and Wisconsin ("Charter school resources," 1995). Despite this recent activity, local teacher unions continue to oppose the development of the concept.

Chester Finn, a conservative research fellow of the Hudson Institute, and his colleagues (1996) warn that any charter school started by unions and bound by collective bargaining agreements and certification requirements could dilute the charter concept. The researchers urge that any charter school "have full control over staff selections, including exemptions from certification rules for employees," contending that "to compromise in this arena is the surest way to strangle an infant charter school in its cradle" (pp. 10–11). Obviously many certified teachers throughout the United States, as well as their unions, have serious disagreements with Finn.

Yet another controversy arises because only a few states require charter schools to make available information regarding student and staff demographics, the number of special needs students served, the number of at-risk and minority students, and staff turnover. As a result, there is widespread suspicion that these schools serve only elite, affluent students (McKinney, 1996).

For these reasons and others, charter school legislation has led to bitter battles between groups proposing new charter schools and local school boards and teachers' unions. These conflicts have led to dozens of lawsuits and countersuits across the country. Dan Diedrich, director of the Horizons Community High School in Wyoming, Michigan (1994), described the problems that faced his school after it became a charter school:

> *The real story . . . is that legislation [in Michigan] was*
> *ill conceived and poorly written, allowing too many*
> *loopholes. The real story is that the Governor is sus-*

pected of having a hidden agenda to aid private schools and destroy the teachers' union. The real story is that seven of the eight Charter Schools nearly died for lack of promised state funds because of a court ruling that declared them unconstitutional. They resorted to bake sales and auctions and appeals for donations. They dismissed custodians and secretaries and asked their teachers to teach without pay. One of the schools had been started on funds secured by the principal from a second mortgage on his house. The funds promised by the state are still being held up in litigation. Horizons was able to survive without resorting to these drastic measures because we had been authorized as a Charter School by our local school district. After we had operated as a successful alternative school for 17 years, our local School Board trusted us enough to carry us through a semester of uncertainty. They paid our bills and eagerly awaited the outcome, along with our Governing Board, of the legal wrangling in the state capitol.

Controversy often accompanies the creation of charter schools. While some schools have enjoyed strong support and uneventful openings, many have not.

For example, in Michigan the charter school experience was interrupted by a lawsuit filed by a Michigan teachers' union, the ACLU, and other civic groups. The key objection was that charter schools "undermine traditional schools by directing badly needed money from them." The director of the Michigan ACLU, Howard Simon, stated, "You don't have to try to privatize public education. Some of this is only helping private schools that are facing hard times . . . all this could be done through the public schools we have." At least two of Michigan's first charter schools reflected many individuals' suspicions that the governor was using the charter school legislation to support private schools. One new charter school was little more than a network of home-school students. Another new charter school, the New Branch Charter School, was a small private school that was able to more than double its previous budget once it obtained charter status (Sanchez, 1995).

In Colorado, the school board of the Denver Public Schools was locked in a battle for more than two years with a group of teachers who proposed a small charter school to be named the Thurgood Marshall Middle School. The issues involved in this controversy, money and control, were no surprise. After the school board turned down the group's charter several times, Cordia Booth, an eighth-grade science teacher in the Denver Public Schools who helped develop the charter proposal, filed a lawsuit against the district, claiming it was breaking the law by ignoring the state legislature's Charter School Bill. The school district countered that the state charter law was unconstitutional because it gave a state body control over a local school board. Booth spent more than $10,000 of her own money for legal fees. She argued that the charter school should receive 94% of the district's $4,500 per-pupil cost, but the district offered only 85%, a percentage larger than the state requirement (80%). Booth maintained that to accept 85% would be to allow blatant discrimination against her anticipated high-risk, minority students ("Charter school resources," 1995).

When the Oregon State Superintendent of Public Education began creating "community schools" around the state that modeled charter schools, the Oregon Education Association, an NEA affiliate, immediately supported two local teachers who brought suit against a local school board. The lawsuit maintained that public money was being used to finance a private school and that the "community school" teachers had no state teaching certification. The suit listed the local board members in the Bend-LaPine School District as defendants because of alleged misuse of public funds. The board members soon were faced with paying their own legal expenses, more than $40,000 after only a few months of litigation. The school district won the first round of litigation, but the decision currently is being appealed. The Oregon Education Association president, Bruce Adams, maintains that the state NEA affiliate does not oppose charter schools but does oppose opening a public school without certified teachers (Carter, 1996).

When the Massachusetts legislature passed a charter school bill, many parents objected that tax money could be taken from their public schools and given to a separate, special school. Parents and educators were concerned that the charter schools were being started and funded to experiment with "untested and potentially detrimental ideas." The president of the Massachusetts Teachers Association was furious. "These schools have been in operation for less than three months," he said, "Yet when you talk to some of the [charter school] people, you think charters have already cured all of the ills of the educational system. We still feel innovation can occur within the system" ("Charter school resources," 1995).

The Massachusetts legislature provided modest interim funding to school districts that lost money to the new charter schools. But the funding was designed only to help each school district make the transition into charter schools; and some districts, including Marblehead, still experienced a shortfall.

Carl Goodman, a lawyer and former town selectman in Marblehead, led a legal challenge to both the local charter school and the state charter law. He argued that charters violated the State Constitution's ban on publicly funding schools that are not "publicly owned and under the exclusive control" of government agents. Goodman also raised concerns regarding the state's effort to control local schools. "Why should the few people who get the ear of a political appointee get a portion of the budget that is otherwise controlled by the elected [town] school committee?" Goodman asked. "If we are to spend several hundred dollars in our town, perhaps the taxpayers would want a say in it" ("Charter school resources," 1995).

Many of the new charters in these and other states have been approved quickly and soon opened for business without conflict. Often, it is not so much the quality of ideas that leads to a quick and easy approval; it may be who is making the proposal.

CHARTER SCHOOL ACHIEVEMENTS

In spite of the controversies and occasional failure of charter schools, most would agree that the states that have passed enabling legislation can be credited with major achievements, especially those states that have given charter schools the greatest degree of freedom. The achievements to date relate to improved student achievement, attendance, and attitudes toward school; positive effects on districts and communities; improved service for at-risk, minority, and special needs students; instructional innovations; and a creative use of public school facilities and funds.

While critics of the charter school movement continue to argue that there are inadequate objective measures to assess charter school student learning and to compare charter school students with public school students, research over the last two decades of alternative schools and magnet schools suggests and predicts that this new form of alternative, the charter school, should have an extensive positive influence on student achievement and student attitudes. And while charter schools are still less than five years old, a number of these distinctive schools have, in fact, reported positive achievement gains. These schools can be found in Minneapolis, Minnesota; Los Angeles and Sacramento, California; Castlerock, Colorado; and elsewhere (Nathan, 1996).

There also is no evidence that charters represent the "end of the world" for public education, as some critics predict. Rather, many charter schools seem to stimulate reforms in the public schools. A school board in Rochester, Minnesota, created their own Montessori public school alternative after a local group proposed to develop a similar school under a charter. In Massachusetts, charter legislation seemed to motivate the Boston Public Schools and the Boston Teachers Union to help teachers create new alternative schools (Myatt & Nathan, 1996). Apparently in response to the Massachusetts charter school legislation, the Boston Public Schools initiated a new program called Pilot Schools. The Pilot Schools program was freed from many local and union regulations and opened only to students in the district. Recently, it was reported that Deborah Meier, founder of the Central Park East Alternative School in New York City and a nationally renowned educator and spokesperson for alternative education, had submitted a proposal to develop a new Pilot School in the Boston Public Schools (Gamble, 1996).

In contrast to fears that charter schools would serve only elite students, several recent studies have documented the fact that charter schools, like the alternative and magnet schools that preceded them, serve large numbers of minority and at-risk youth. A study by the Hudson Institute in January 1996 found that minority and disabled students and their parents were "flocking" to charter schools (Finn, Bierlein, & Manno, 1996). In six states with the largest number of charter schools, Louann Bierlein, of Louisiana State University, found that minority students constituted over 40% of charter school enrollments (17% African American, 15% Hispanic, 5% Native American, and 3%

Asian), though those minorities constituted only 31% of the students in regular public schools in those states (Finn et al., 1996). In 1995 a survey by the Education Commission of the States and Center for School Change found that about half of the charter schools then in operation were designed specifically to serve at-risk youth.

During every debate over charter schools, someone inevitably claims that charter schools allow some special interest or religious group to attain public funding in order to teach their particular ideas. With the exception of the one group of electronically networked home schoolers who gained a charter in Michigan, there have been no other examples of this. And the Michigan home-schooling charter immediately attracted a lawsuit that led to a redefinition of charter school legislation. As the Hudson Institute researchers found:

> *The charter world is marvelously varied and we do not necessarily agree with the educational philosophy or the curriculum of every school we have encountered. But we have seen none that seem outside the pale of defensible (and in many respects familiar) educational thought and practice. We haven't stumbled on any witchcraft schools or Klan schools, for example. Perhaps the most far-out versions we have spotted are a couple of virtual schools that use modern technology to bring instructional resources to students . . . who are not physically on the premises. In fact, most of the charter schools we have seen can be described either as variants on progressives and "educational thought" or versions of traditional education (with some interesting efforts to blend the two)* (Finn et al., 1996, p. 2).

A review of charter schools reveals a wide spectrum of distinctive themes. Many have concluded that charter schools seem to be far more creative and innovative than the high-profile schools created by design teams sponsored by the New America Schools Development Corporation (Finn et al., 1996). The reason for this may be that charter schools are a grassroots phenomenon. Many of the charters are, in fact, previous alternative public schools with years of experience behind them. Finally, charter schools are far more likely to have been planned around someone's kitchen table than in a superintendent's office or the school board room.

Like the alternative schools and magnet schools that preceded them, charter schools are demonstrating how high-quality education can be practiced in modest or unusual facilities. Most charter schools operate in what could charitably be called minimal facilities. The buildings tend to be old, dilapidated, crowded, and sometimes temporary; and they commonly lack auditoriums, gyms, playgrounds, well-equipped labs, media centers, and lunch rooms (Finn et al., 1996). Yet there is a passion found in the teachers, students, and parents, a team spirit of dedication and determination. All of those involved in charter schools are there because they choose to be, and they are all "shareholders in the dream." Perhaps even more important, charter schools are demonstrating remarkable new ways to allocate funding. By renting facilities, using diversified staffing, and often eliminating administrative positions, charters have far greater flexibility with their funding to meet the specific needs of their students.

IMPROVING CHARTER SCHOOLS

In the midst of continuing struggles between local public schools, teachers' unions, and new charter schools, there is a growing consensus that charters are here to stay and will continue to increase. Certainly President Clinton's endorsement, accompanied by the call for increased federal funds, will add to this growth. There is also a renewed interest in improving charter school legislation. Legislators who were involved in passing charter school legislation in the various states have made five major recommendations for improving charter schools:

- Provide charter schools the same per-pupil allocation as other public schools. (Most states fund charter schools with less per-pupil cost than the state average.)

- Permit more than one organization to sponsor charter schools. (Almost all of the legislators agreed that local school boards should not be the only authorizing agency for charters.)

- Eliminate the "cap" on the number of charter schools. (Most states specify the number of charter schools that can be established; some states have reached that maximum number, and the waiting lists are growing.)

- Private charter schools should be as independent as possible.

- Charter schools should be provided with start-up funds. (Most of the legislators surveyed believed charter schools should have the same start-up funds as any other public school receives) (Center for School Change, 1996).

Others acknowledge the importance of the five issues raised by the legislators yet place the key importance on a freedom to hire and fire personnel and to decide independently on the use of certified or noncertified teachers.

HOW TO START A CHARTER SCHOOL

After all of the news stories about the horrible conflicts, battles, and lawsuits surrounding charter schools, we were very apprehensive about developing a charter proposal. After talking to several people who had start-

ed charter schools, we changed our minds. For what we were able to achieve, the process was really not that difficult. Our charter school is worth everything *that we had to do . . . and none of us would ever consider going back to teaching in a regular public school classroom.*

Teacher,
California

You want to know how to start a charter school? Well, I can tell you. First you get a really good lawyer and next you start raising money for your own defense fund.

Teacher,
Colorado

An effort to start a charter school, even in states where enabling legislation has been passed, is a formidable task, especially in major metropolitan areas. The process demands commitment from the "founders" to accept responsibility for being school owners and for starting an educational "small business," accompanied by a variety of legal obligations and liabilities. At its worst, starting a charter school can involve years of litigation, expensive legal fees, the possible loss of professional protections, and even giving up state retirement programs.

The best advice for starting a charter school comes from a national survey conducted by Joe Nathan and his colleagues at the Hubert Humphrey Center for School Change at the University of Minnesota. In a survey of 110 charter schools in seven states, conducted in the spring of 1995, a comprehensive set of specific issues were identified that are significant in the creation of a charter school.

Check out the situation and get accurate information. The first thing to do is call the state superintendent of public education or perhaps a local school district and find out whether charter school legislation has been passed in the state. If not, you might explore whether there are other state or local programs that have been established that reflect the charter concept. Proponents of charter schools should find out if there are alternative schools or magnet schools in the local school district and in the state. Charter proponents should request information from each of these schools. It is also important to check out the attitude of local school boards, superintendents, and collective bargaining units toward charters. Charter proponents should ask how many charters have been established and if there is a state limitation on the number of charters. If charter legislation has been passed, it is important to find out who introduced the legislation and to get to know that legislator.

Read the small print. It is essential that the charter school information and the legislative action regarding charter schools be reviewed carefully. Anyone who is seriously considering developing a charter school should determine who can apply for charter status, who authorizes new charters, whether certified teachers must be employed, what the appropriate process involves, and whether the charter school legislation is a "weak" or "strong" piece of legislation. Charter proponents also need to learn the per-pupil cost of public education in the state and local school district and the percent of the per-pupil cost that will be allocated to a charter school. It is important to understand the relationship to and authority of the local school board. Some states establish the local school board as the only authorizing agency. In other states, the state board of education or other new agencies have been established to authorize charters. Some states permit more than one authorizing agency.

Read between the lines. A careful review of charter school legislation will help groups and individuals anticipate the kinds and complexity of problems likely to be encountered. If certified teachers are not used, it is all but certain that the state collective bargaining unit is likely to file suit against any proposed charter. If charter schools can be authorized only by a local school board, it is possible that authority and control issues could prove to be difficult. On the other hand, some local school districts have served as a safety net to assist charters until funds are transferred from the state and until legal battles have been resolved.

Straight from the horse's mouth. It also is essential to talk to others in the state who have applied for charter status or who have been approved for charter school status. No one will be more helpful regarding what to watch out for, what to avoid, who to trust, etc. There are centers and information sources available in some states, as well as national information centers. (See the appendices for charter school resources.)

Get a good attorney or seek out legal advice. Because of the complexities of starting a charter school, it is essential that those proposing the charter find good legal assistance to review the charter legislation and to provide advice and counsel. If an individual or group cannot afford a private attorney, there are legal-aid services in most cities in the United States and often attorneys who will provide their assistance on a pro bono basis.

Check out a small-business assistance center. Since the majority of all new small businesses fail within the first two years, charter school proponents should seek out business assistance. Most community colleges, some universities, and occasionally even local Chambers of Commerce have "Small-Business Assistance Centers," "Family Business Assistance Centers," or "Small-Business Incubation Centers" to advise, consult with, and assist new small businesses and to help them develop a business plan. It is essential that every charter school develop and use a business plan. Since most teachers have little or no business expertise, a small-business assistance center should prove invaluable in helping to develop a business plan and to guide the creation of a new charter school. If no assistance center is available, seek assistance from local business leaders, accountants, or the Chamber of Commerce.

Try to avoid a David/Goliath struggle. To ensure that proponents of a charter school do not step immediately into a crushing legal battle with a local school board or teachers' union, every effort should be made to develop positive relationships with these two groups. If not, charter proponents must realize the kind of opposition they are likely to face and consider whether it is worth the cost and time involved. If positive relationships are possible, many good things can occur. Both a school district and a teachers' union can be of enormous help in supporting a new charter if accommodations can be made to work together. Both school districts and teachers' unions have lawyers, accountants, and business administrators that charters could access through some type of subcontract. Yet charter school founders need to weigh carefully the loss of autonomy that these services may bring.

Seek out strong, influential allies. Many new charters are former alternative schools with long years of experience, success, and leadership. Finding teachers, parents, school administrators, and business leaders who are well known and influential is extremely important in establishing positive attitudes toward the charter. Often, area business leaders have proven invaluable in assisting and advising charter schools; sometimes it is a former superintendent, retired principal, or respected local teacher who will bring acceptance and positive support. A number of new charters have been developed in cooperation with a college, university, or social agency. Once again, these allies can provide consultation regarding legal, business, and personnel issues and administrative processes and can serve as powerful advocates.

Don't forget the nitty-gritty: retirement, health insurance, liability. Since many of the charter school staff will have been former teachers, it is essential to gain a clear understanding of the opportunities (or lack of) to affiliate with state employee retirement and group health insurance programs. Charter school owners also must obtain exact information regarding liability responsibilities. These issues must not be overlooked, for they are absolutely essential in providing new owners and new employees a clear understanding of the risks, safeguards, and challenges they may face. And while most education regulations have been waived for charters, these new schools are not exempt from health, fire, earthquake, and other safety codes.

Make friends with the media. The media usually are quite interested in alternative, magnet, and charter schools. These schools are new, quite different, and often involved in creative activities, unusual programs, and sometimes difficult battles. Get to know education reporters, TV anchors, and local radio personalities. Invite them to the school. Supply them with good story lines or hot tips. The media can be a strong, positive ally in the creation of a new charter.

Strive for autonomy. Depending on the state's charter legislation, a new charter school may have almost total autonomy or be little more than a neighborhood school empowered with site-based management. Charter school proponents not only should work to get approved and funded, they also must work to gain the maximum amount of authority that they can obtain. The greater the autonomy, the greater the possibilities of success. If charter schools are to be held accountable for student learning, the school must have authority over hiring, personnel issues, and curriculum. A charter school must establish a local governing board with as much policy-making authority as possible.

Take student achievement seriously. Because the future of a charter school depends on documenting student achievement, charters must be careful to negotiate the specific terms and responsibilities of this important issue. Will an external, standardized test be required? What form of school-based testing, assessment, and evaluation will occur? Charters must find expert advice on authentic assessment, mastery learning, and goal-based education.

In 1995, a survey of 110 charter schools found that student achievement was being documented with a wide variety of methods: standardized national achievement tests, statewide assessment tests, and various forms of "performance measures," including portfolio assessment, parent surveys, student interviews, and behavioral indicators (Nathan, 1995). Charter schools often can turn to colleges and universities or to regional education laboratories for assistance in developing and implementing an appropriate and effective assessment program.

It also is essential that the charter school is given sufficient time to increase student learning. This is not a quick process. Some states give charter schools three years to document their success, other states provide five years. Anything less than three years is unrealistic.

Don't forget start-up costs. After battling through the intricate maze of legal, educational, and business issues and surviving the sometimes brutal in-fighting and political warfare that can surround charter schools, the leader of a group who is finally authorized to develop and operate a charter school then must face an all-but-crushing problem: there are usually no start-up funds. Equally as difficult, most states do not provide state aid until the school is open, students are selected, and the school year is under way. State reimbursement usually does not occur until one or two months after the school has been in operation. While charters usually can operate quite well on a part of the state or local per-pupil cost, the task of securing a facility, developing printed brochures and public relations information, conducting school and curriculum development efforts, and training or re-training teachers is enormous and expensive.

Some new charter school leaders have financed these efforts from securing a second mortgage on their homes or have used credit cards or lines of credit to cover the start-up costs. Others have sought donations or held fund-raising activities. Some charters charge students a "fee"; and most develop proposals to local, private, or corporate foundations. In the end, the group who proposed and developed the charter school will invest huge amounts of "sweat equity" to get the new school up and running. Teachers, parents, students, and interested volunteers will invest thousands of hours in finding and refurbishing a building and checking out fire codes, health codes, and access requirements. They often even help modify the building themselves, find furniture, and obtain donations for technology, textbooks, reference books, and other instructional materials (Nathan, 1995).

Recently, the federal government significantly increased the funding for charter schools. Funding rose from $6 million in fiscal year 1994 to $18 million in 1996 to $51 million in 1997. And charter schools may face an even better financial future. Current federal funding is focused on one-time start-up costs because, at this time, the lack of this support appears to be the greatest documented need. Nineteen states already have received federal funds and are likely to see these funds increased. The other six states with charter legislation may be able to obtain funds through competitive grants. The funding and the enhanced visibility of charters during the presidential campaign of 1996 will surely encourage other states to further explore the idea.

CONCLUSION

Even though all charter schools have been in operation for only five years or less, there exists sufficient evidence to draw a number of significant conclusions:

First, charter schools are here to stay. Given the growing support and funding from the federal government, widespread media attention, and increasing interest throughout the nation, it seems fair to conclude that charter schools will not go away. As one proponent stated, "They will never get this genie back in the bottle." In fact, the number of states approving charters is likely to continue to grow, as are the number of proposals being developed for charters and the number of charters being approved. During the next few years, some states that originally established a cap on the number of charters probably will expand the number that can be in operation or perhaps even open the opportunity to unlimited numbers. Some of the states that passed "weak" charter legislation are under pressure to revise their original legislation. States in which statewide authorizing agencies approve charter proposals will have more charter schools than states in which local school boards perform this function. Federal funding will provide start-up funds for charters; and some states are likely to begin providing low-cost, long-term loans to help initiate charter schools.

Second, charter schools have a positive effect on other public schools. These schools will provide a powerful stimulus for school districts to change. There seems to be real value in this type of educational competition.

Third, teachers' unions will need to find common ground with charter schools. Even though the idea of providing public education without certified teachers is simply anathema to teacher unions, there will be far too many union members who want to start charter schools and work in them for the unions to stand in opposition. Also, public opinion and subsequent political pressure are not likely to permit such opposition.

Fourth, the battles over charter schools are likely to continue. Given the issues of money, control, and collective bargaining agreements that are at the heart of the charter school wars, there is no reason to believe that the struggles will just go away. As more states pass charter legislation, there will be more legal challenges, political struggles, and efforts to halt or slow charter school development.

Fifth, there is a need for statewide technical assistance centers to provide teacher training, technical assistance, and business consultation. These centers could establish support networks of charter and alternative schools and coordinate a program in which teachers from established charter schools can help other teachers and groups who are proposing schools.

After five years, charter schools appear to be firmly established. These schools and programs complement the legion of alternative and magnet schools currently providing choice and more appropriate services to the youth of the nation. As public schools continue their quest to teach all students, charter schools will play an increasingly important and significant role.

REFERENCES

Carter, S. (1996, October 27). Learning the new way: Bend Community School's novel curriculum draws compliments, criticisms. *Sunday Oregonian*, pp. C1, C11.

Center for School Change. (1996). CSC asked to present new charter school report at national conferences. *Fine Print: A Careful Look at School Reform, 5* (1), 5.

Charter school resources: Breaking away: The charter school revolution. (1995, November 29). *Education Week Special Report*, p. 15.

Diedrich, D. (1994, May). Principal's editorial column. *Horizons Community High School News*.

Education Commission of the States and Center for School Change. (1995). *Charter schools: What are they up to? A 1995 survey.* Denver: Authors.

Finn, C.E., Bierlein, L.A., & Manno, B.V. (1996). *Charter schools in action: A first look.* Washington, DC: Hudson Institute Educational Excellence Network, Charter Schools in Action Project.

Gamble, C. (1996, October 16). Meier submits proposal to run Boston pilot school. *Education Week*, p. 5.

Gregory, T. (1993). *Making high schools work: Lessons from the open school.* New York: Teachers College Press.

McKinney, J.R. (1996). Charter schools: A new barrier for children with disabilities. *Educational Leadership, 54* (2), 22–25.

Molnar, A. (1996). Charter schools: The smiling face of disinvestment. *Educational Leadership, 54* (2), 9–15.

Myatt, L., & Nathan, L. (1996, September). One school's journey in the Age of Reform. *Phi Delta Kappan*, 78, 24–25.

Nathan, J. (1995). *Charter public schools: A brief history and preliminary lessons.* Minneapolis: Center for School Change, Hubert Humphrey Institute of Public Affairs, University of Minnesota.

Nathan, J. (1996, September). Possibilities, problems, and progress: Early lessons from the charter movement. *Phi Delta Kappan, 78*, 18–23.

Romer, R. (1993). Charter schools: A tool for reinventing public education. *Changing Schools, 21* (3), 1–9.

Sanchez, R. (1995, January 9–15). Michigan tries teaching a new lesson. *Washington Post Weekly*, p. 31.

Wilt, J. (1993). Charter schools: An entrepreneurial approach to public schools. *Changing Schools, 21* (3), 10–12.

8

Alternative Schools: Solutions for Lasting Reform

I F WE HAVE LEARNED ANYTHING in the past two decades, it is what is wrong with public education. Ask any bored junior or senior high school student in America and, if you will listen, he or she will let you know. Public education is too removed from life, too removed from the issues that matter to kids today. Too many schools continue to focus on the 20% of students who will graduate from college and ill serve the other 80%. While society has experienced incredible social, technical, and economic change over the past 30 years, public schools have remained far too static and have been left behind. Public education must change.

Public education must abandon education programs that do not motivate children and youth to establish significant goals for their lives, that do not strive for excellence, and provide equitable educational opportunities for all. States must abandon their reliance on property taxes for funding public education, a practice which perpetuates a tragic educational and economic apartheid on American youth. Public education must abandon the idea that a single curriculum will serve the complex needs of our diverse student body. Public education must recognize the bankruptcy of the practice of equating learning with a prescribed number of hours and days in required courses, with grades, courses, and transcripts. Public education must abandon the Carnegie unit, that outdated artifact of a world that no longer exists. Public education must abandon the practices of ignoring personal teaching and learning styles and assigning students to specific schools, programs, and curricula based on street addresses. Public education must abandon the idea that learning can occur only inside a classroom, at a particular time of day, in a prescribed set of minutes, with a group of 25 to 30 students. Public education must abandon the idea that knowledge comes prepackaged in textbooks that reflect isolated disciplines. Public education must break up the huge, impersonal junior and senior high schools and replace the "General Motors" model of education with the "Saturn team" approach.

We no longer can justify our system because it works well for some of the students—students who undoubtedly would succeed in spite of what public education provides. We know what is wrong with public education; we also know what can be done.

The problem with acting on ideas for reform has always been that public education is so big, so complex, so regulated, so steeped in tradition, and so fragmented into thousands of locally controlled school districts, that effective change on a national or on a state level is virtually impossible. Certainly, states can add graduation requirements and mandate testing programs, but the cultures of schools have rarely been significantly altered by such laws, mandates, and requirements. Unless teachers and parents want to change, change simply will not occur. People cannot be legislated to abandon their comfortable, established approaches to teaching and learning in favor of the unfamiliar, even threatening world of the unknown.

Researchers have documented that changing an existing school with an established faculty can involve a five- to seven-year process of consensus building, even when the school has already been moving toward improvement. And even after the consensus-building years, there will still be teachers in any school who do not share the emerging consensus and must be given the opportunity to transfer to another school with which their philosophies are more compatible. Changing existing schools is almost always a long and challenging process. In fact, we know that some existing schools probably cannot be changed.

But compared to changing an existing school, establishing an alternative school is a far easier, more positive experience. Planning for a new school can take as little as one year, and the challenges, while still significant, are of a fundamentally different nature. The alternative school concept provides an effective method for restructuring education, because it embraces competing visions of reform and involves only those teachers, parents, and students who support the idea of change.

AN ENDURING EDUCATIONAL CONCEPT: ALTERNATIVE SCHOOLS

First appearing in the late 1960s in a dozen communities across the nation, unusual, innovative public schools began to spring up and become available to parents, students, and teachers on the basis of choice. At the time, no book had been written about alternative schools; in fact, no one had yet even coined the term. There was no program in the federal government supporting and disseminating information about alternative schools; there was no information diffusion network. None of the great foundations had discovered alternative schools; there was no high-profile funding program to support these small programs. It was truly a grassroots movement that began a "quiet revolution."

Each step of the way, these alternative schools had to battle for their survival and integrity. At first, they were discounted as "counterculture" schools for the disadvantaged, disruptive, and disengaged students whom they served. "Hippie schools" they were sometimes called, and then dismissed as too radical for public education. Most felt that the only real value in alternative schools was that they provided a place to send the disruptive students who made their classrooms so chaotic. Later, alternative schools were disparaged as a "gimmick" of the federal government, designed to trick parents of different racial groups into sending their children to school together. Alternative schools were accused of not being "serious" schools. Schools in hospitals, television stations, banks, and museums? Did anyone really believe that this was a substitute for serious classroom learning? And what about charter schools? Schools without lengthy regulations? Schools with limited required courses? Schools without certified teachers? Many branded them as just another education fad that would come and go.

But in spite of considerable adversity, alternative schools survived and flourished. Over time, the success of alternative public schools could not be discounted. Public education found it "needed" alternative schools; legislatures mandated them. Slowly, almost methodically, alternative schools endured, increased, and began to show up everywhere, quietly growing inside the shadow of public education. These schools firmly established themselves in districts and communities.

Today they stand, gaining strength and influence with integrity. Alternative educators have quietly demonstrated again and again that students in alternative schools achieve more than they did in their prior schools; they have more positive attitudes; they attend school more regularly; they drop out less frequently; they are far less violent and disruptive; and they show dramatic gains in how they perceive learning and themselves. Alternative schools work for students, their teachers, parents, and communities.

Researchers have spent the past 30 years studying why alternatives are this effective, why they work so well with all types of students, why they succeed in both rural and urban locations. Their conclusion: Alternative schools demonstrate these advantages over traditional schools because they create small, caring communities of support for teachers and students.

Alternative education—whether it is through a single alternative school, a cluster of schools within a school, a network of urban magnet schools, a statewide residential academy, or a charter school—creates small, supportive, caring communities that bond teachers, students, and their parents. Students in alternative schools know and care for one another. Like members of a quality athletic team, they provide "assists"; they work to help and support one another. Students are surrounded by adults who care and advocate for them, hold high expectations for excellence, and help them develop personal goals for their lives and career paths for the future. This type of nurturing support is exactly what so many students need and so often are denied in most other public schools.

THE SOLUTION: ALTERNATIVE SCHOOLS

To borrow a commercial motto, public education needs to "just do it!" All the tools for creating lasting reform are in place. Alternative schools have a solid research base and a 30-year track record of success. A significant inventory of educational models has been tested. Assistance centers and support networks are available. Educators, legislators, and parents have learned how to plan, develop, and implement alternative schools. They have learned how to recruit teachers, students, and parents, how to develop curricula that relate to the needs and interests of the students, and how to diversify teaching and learning through individual self-study, small-group investigations, individualized self-paced learning, computer-assisted instruction, and community-based learning experiences. Effective assessments for student learning have been developed and utilized. Thousands of districts have successful alternative and magnet schools that welcome visitation, and 25 states offer charter schools and many have set up networks for their support.

Using alternative education as an approach to reform ensures that all schools, whether the local neighborhood school or the large comprehensive junior/senior high school, are available for those who support and select them. Parents and students may choose to attend a large junior or senior high school with a marching band, an intercollegiate athletic program, and sophisticated science and language labs, but others may choose career-based theme schools or small schools for self-directed and experiential learning. Alternative education provides the model for all of these very different schools to exist side by side, each supported by their own advocates. Over time, some schools will lose their support and they will close, while other concepts will be the basis for new schools. Alternative education provides for an ongoing, built-in method for continuing educational evolution.

Students, parents, and communities must demand and develop additional alternative schools. Business leaders must require the diversification of the local public schools through magnet schools with career themes. Teachers, parents, and business leaders must make a concerted effort to establish and improve charter legislation, and expand the number of charter schools that can be developed. Legislators must continue to create and support policy that encourages and nurtures alternative education. Teachers, parents, and business leaders in every state must work to influence the teacher organizations and unions, to nudge their considerable power into the support of alternative, magnet, and charter schools. Citizens must contact their school boards, superintendents, legislators, and teachers' union representatives and encourage all of them to support education alternatives.

As a nation, we simply cannot afford, nor should we tolerate, a system of public education that fails to educate a substantial number of our youth. We have the solution for lasting reform—alternative schools—and we must use it.

Appendix I

Frequently Asked Questions Regarding Alternative Schools

Should communities develop a school within a school or an alternative at a separate site?

Highly successful alternative schools can be found as both schools within schools and as stand-alone programs. There are advantages and disadvantages to each. Some alternative educators explain that regardless of which type of school is developed, each has a unique set of problems. A school within a school has the advantage of enabling students to take part in the larger school. Students can use the library and cafeteria, take a course outside of the alternative, etc. Unfortunately, close proximity of two very different approaches to education often generates friction, antagonism, and jealousy between students and teachers alike. Regardless, a school within a school must have a clearly defined area with attractive signs and facilities.

An alternative located at an off-campus site has several advantages and disadvantages. For at-risk students, there is great value in going to school someplace other than the building where they often have had so much trouble. An off-campus location can provide the insulation and protective environment at-risk students need and can help to generate the esprit de corps that is so important to the success of an alternative. Establishing an alternative school for at-risk youth at a community college or university has even greater value. And if the school has a curriculum or career theme, the school location becomes one of the most important aspects of the program. For students interested in health professions to actually go to school in a hospital has powerful motivational effects on learning. The same is true for students interested in performing arts going to school at a theater, or students interested in the environment attending school at a nature center. However, the task of finding a facility that meets educational standards can often pose difficult and expensive problems. The problem of obtaining equipment and instructional aids, gaining access to a library, or even arranging for lunch on site can often prove difficult.

Some would argue that neither of these approaches is satisfactory, that both tend to isolate and stigmatize the alternative students. These educators believe that dividing up an entire school into a number of alternative clusters or creating an entire range of systemwide magnets is a far better idea. Because every student or school system in the school is some type of alternative program, the isolation and stigma are eliminated, as are the "us and them" type of jealousies. There are a number of superb examples of these types of programs. At the high school level, the widely acclaimed Central Park East houses four separate programs in one building. The same is true of the GEM elementary school in Florida.

Districtwide alternatives can be found in Houston, Dallas, Los Angeles, and other cities. Houston enrolls more than 25% of its students in alternative/magnet schools. Many middle-level schools also are dividing entire schools into interdisciplinary teams consisting of small groups of teachers and students.

Do alternative schools cost more?

The answer is yes and no. Almost all alternative schools need start-up funds to establish a program and get it under way. There are always funds needed for teacher training, printing and advertising, planning, development, evaluation, and even for furniture, equipment, and instructional aides. Also, there often is an added cost to school districts for transportation and facilities rental.

After these initial costs, many alternative schools operate on exactly the same per-pupil cost as all other programs in the district. This also is true for charter schools. Of course, because of the way charter schools are funded, they are able to use very creative financing that often provides more money for instruction and far less for administration.

Over the years, many alternative educators have come to conclude that the only way to ensure the creation and long-term success of an alternative is to use regular district funding formulas. Too often, alternatives that are started with external funds are closed when the funds run out, or the school finds that it is unable to offer the same type of program that was available while the external funds were being used.

By their very nature, some alternatives do cost more money. Many states provide added formula funding for school districts that create alternative schools for at-risk children and youth. In the same way that some people need intensive health care, some students need highly individualized, intensive educational care. Most of the career academies or special-theme magnet schools cost more simply because of the need for special equipment or special educational materials. The good news is that many of the special-theme schools have partnerships with business and industry, which make donations to meet these special instructional needs.

When planning an alternative school, cost projections must be related to the specific kind of school that is being developed.

How big should an alternative school be?

As described in chapter three, the small size of alternative schools is one of the primary reasons for their remarkable success. Research has documented the negative influence of large comprehensive schools on certain students and the positive benefits for teachers and students working in a small school. Small school size contributes to esprit de corps and helps to establish the unique, personalized school environment that is so powerful in teaching and learning.

However, there is a problem in creating an alternative school that is too small. The school must be big enough to support a collection of teachers sufficient to deliver the desired educational program. The average size of alternative schools in the United States is approximately 150 to 250 students. Most believe an alternative should have no more than 400 students in order to be effective.

When planning an alternative school, set a limit on the number of students and be prepared to start a waiting list.

Is the goal of an alternative school to "transition" students as soon as possible back into the mainstream school?

There is a widely held, though erroneous belief that alternative schools should serve to "fix kids up" as soon as possible, to get them straightened out and back to the regular school program.

While returning to the regular school program always should be an option for students, this cannot be the goal. So many students, both those at risk and those who are motivated, would suffer negative consequences should they be returned arbitrarily to a regular program. For at-risk youth, it has taken many years for them to develop the problems associated with learning, and no alternative school will correct these problems quickly. For the highly motivated student, a return to a conventional program can lead to frustration, boredom, and often defiance. Research and evaluation have documented that many students drop out if they are simply returned to a regular school program.

Isn't alternative education simply a sophisticated form of tracking?

Research has focused on the great power associated with students and parents choosing to participate in alternative schools. Students become invested in learning and motivated by volunteering for an alternative. Also, since the students are surrounded by caring and demanding teachers with high expectations who choose to be in a particular program, student learning tends to increase, often significantly. Most tracking programs have low expectations for the "slower" track and usually staff these programs with teachers who do not want to be there, often beginning teachers with little experience. Tracking leads to negative self-concept and poor achievement for at-risk youth. Alternative schools have just the opposite effect.

Many alternative schools work hard to ensure that their programs attract all kinds of students. Some go even further and establish "quotas" so that a very heterogeneous mix of students is ensured.

Do alternative schools stigmatize students?

Sometimes, alternative schools do tend to isolate and stigmatize students. This is especially true if a community has only one type of alternative school and that particular program is for at-risk youth. Sometimes, school districts seem to create alternative schools so they can get the most difficult kids out of their schools and classrooms. When this happens, everyone knows that the alternative school is a type of "dumping ground." Some school districts have alternative programs in such old and shabby facilities that the buildings themselves establish a negative tone. It is not alternative education that stigmatizes youth, it is the motives and practices of the school district. If the alternative school is housed in an attractive facility, outstanding teachers are selected for the staff, students choose to attend, and a mix of students is attracted to the program, there should be no negative stigma attached to attending the alternative.

Should the focus of a new alternative school be on replicating an established alternative model, or should a group of parents, teachers, administrators, and students create their own unique approach?

First of all, every group of parents, teachers, administrators, and students who plans and develops an alternative school tends to create a unique program. It is absolutely essential that those who plan an alternative school design their own, personal, "perfect school" and ensure that, to a reasonable degree, the vision of the school is shared by all. Consensus is absolutely essential in developing an effective alternative school. Even if an established model—such as a Montessori, a school without walls, or a performing arts school—is used, it is essential that a local planning group develop a school that reflects their own unique ideas and that represents the community in which they live.

However, there is great value in using an established model as a basis for a new school. The planning team can visit a school similar to the one they wish to start. They can develop networks of support and obtain consultants and advice. Established models often are less threatening and easier to market in a community. Few people could recognize a school called the Downtown Learning Academy or the Hawthorne Center; almost everyone would recognize a Montessori school.

If alternative schools are available in the school district, won't all the more sophisticated students and their parents choose the alternatives, thus "dumbing down" the conventional schools?

When school districts develop multiple alternative schools or magnet programs, care must be taken to ensure that the more educated parents do not select the more attractive programs, leaving poor, less sophisticated parents and students at the conventional school. This can be done by providing free transportation for all students, providing information and orientation programs for all parents, and establishing quotas at the alternative schools to ensure a comprehensive, heterogeneous mix of students. Most large urban school districts require each alternative and magnet school to have ethnic, geographic, and gender balances in the program that reflect the local community. Two recent studies have demonstrated that alternative and magnet schools serve diverse student populations.

Why do local school boards and superintendents oppose charter schools?

Public school proponents fear that if charter schools are unchecked, they will drain money from public schools and educate only the upper echelon of students. They fear that the charter will draw the best students from the other public schools. They also worry about losing control of public education in their jurisdiction.

Can charter schools pick and choose the students they want?

Because charter schools usually specialize, they attract certain kinds of students. They may target at-risk youth, students who excel with technology, or inner-city children. However, they cannot discriminate based on sex, religion, or race; and they must consider any student who applies.

What would prevent a private school from declaring itself a charter school and demanding public money?

Most charter laws prevent existing private schools from becoming charter schools. A charter school cannot be based on religion, although it can teach about religion just as public schools do.

If charter schools are independent, what assurance is there that they will not squander public money?

Charter school contracts call for school audits and detailed financial reporting to the sponsor. Yet mismanagement of tax dollars remains a concern of educators and legislators alike.

Can charter schools teach anything they want?

Yes and no. They generally are free to design their own curriculum; but most states require students to perform at or above average on standardized tests, so the schools must emphasize core subjects.

Why do teachers' unions often oppose charter schools?

Many of the states have passed charter legislation that does not require the use of certified teachers. Unions and many public school educators see this as both a "quality" issue and as an anti-union technique. Many teachers' unions fear a significant reallocation of state and district funds that will negatively affect traditional programs.

Appendix II

Alternative Schools Research-Based Evaluation Criteria

STUDENT ACCESS

1. Do students choose to participate in the school?

2. Are there established criteria for admitting students to the school?

3. Does the school use the criteria in admitting students?

4. Do students and parents participate in an orientation program prior to attending the school?

5. Does the school provide information/orientation for junior high and high school principals and counselors?

6. What role do junior high and high school principals and counselors play in the school referrals and admissions?

7. Are students ever turned down for admission?

8. Are students ever assigned to the school?

9. Do students and parents sign a contract prior to admission to the school?

10. If a student leaves the school, is there a plan for re-admission?

CARING AND DEMANDING STAFF

11. Have the principal and the teachers chosen to work in the school?

12. Do the principals and teachers have specific backgrounds or training to prepare them to work effectively with the student population?

13. Are teachers free to transfer to another school if they are dissatisfied?

14. Are noncertified teachers used in special school programs?

15. Are there criteria for recruiting teachers to the school? Are parents, students, and teachers involved in recruiting and interviewing potential teachers?

16. Do teachers appear to care for students and hold high expectations for all students?

CURRICULUM

17. Is the school curriculum designed to meet the needs of the student body?

18. Does the school provide for individualized learning?

19. Does the school provide for competency-based learning?

20. Does the school use learning contracts?

21. Does the school emphasize the development of self-concept and self-esteem?

22. Does the school provide a way to "catch up" if students are far behind in graduation credits?

23. Does the school use the GED as a graduation option?

24. Does the school complement classroom teaching and learning with other learning opportunities?

25. Does the school use learning incentives to motivate students?

26. If students lack basic skills, does the school have a program to address this need?

27. Does the school provide one-to-one tutoring?

28. Does the school provide adult mentors?

29. Does the school have a peer mentor program?

30. Does the school complement academic study with vocational, technical, and career study?

31. Does the school involve the students in community internships?

32. Does the school involve students in community service activities (tutoring younger students, leading field trips for younger students, providing service in nursing homes, hospitals, etc.)?

33. Does the school carefully assess student learning and academic development?

34. Does the school conduct follow-up evaluations of graduates and of dropouts?

35. Does the school use technology as a significant part of the teaching/learning process?

36. Do students use computers in their learning?

37. Do students graduate with computer and technology competencies?

SCHOOL ORGANIZATION/STRUCTURE/SIZE

38. May students attend the school either full- or part-time?

39. Does the school have an evening program or is there an evening program available to the students?

40. Does the school provide an extended-day schedule?

41. Does the school have a summer program or is a summer program available to the students?

42. Does the school have a partnership with a local business or industry?

43. Does the school have partners who volunteer in the school?

44. Does the school serve fewer than 400 students, fewer than 250 students, fewer than 150 students?

45. Do the teachers and students seem to form a positive learning community?

46. Is the school accredited by the state department of education or a national association?

SOCIAL SERVICES

47. Does the school complement academic studies with other types of social-service programs:

   - Drug and Alcohol Prevention Programs
   - Parenting Programs

- Child Care Programs
- Counseling Programs
- Self-Esteem-Building Activities

48. Does the school assist students with accessing social services (food, food stamps, housing, transportation, etc.)?

49. Does the school assist students with health services?

50. Does the school use some type of youth services council or community committee to coordinate access to community social services?

51. Does the school provide child care?

52. Does the school provide health services for infants?

53. Does the school provide teen-parent programs?

54. Does the school provide parenting classes for the parents of the students?

CAREER/VOCATIONAL/TECHNICAL

55. Does the school have a formal program of career exploration and awareness?

56. Does the school participate in a career fair? A college fair?

57. Is the school involved in a 2 + 2 or Tech Prep Program?

58. Is the school involved in a partnership with a local JPTA or a business roundtable?

59. Does the school have vocational and technical internships? Apprenticeships?

60. Can students attend local community colleges part-time while in high school?

61. Can students access a Job Corps Training Center?

62. Can students receive college credit for courses taken in high school?

63. Does the school have a school-to-work program?

64. Does the school have a work-experience program?

Appendix III

Alternative School Support Organizations

Frank Andrew
West Virginia Department of Education
Capitol Complex, Bldg. #6, Room B252
1900 Kanawha Blvd., East
Charleston, WV 25305-0330
(304) 558-2240

Jane B. Ansley, Executive Director
Washington Alternative Learning Association (WALA)
PO Box 795
Port Townsend, WA 98368
(360) 385-9252

Sandy Bell, President
Texas Association for Alternative Education
Academy of Creative Education
5810 Blanco Road
San Antonio, TX 78216
(210) 257-2227

Sandra Blair, Director of Alternative Schools
Georgia Department of Education
Twin Towers East
205 Butler Street
Atlanta, GA 30334
(404) 656-3074

Marcia Boney, President
Georgia Association for Alternative Education
Brunswick High School
3920 Habersham Street
Brunswick, GA 31523
(912) 261-3876

Chris Burge, Education Specialist
Department of Education
Gordon Persons Building
50 North Ripley Street
Montgomery, AL 36130-3901
(334) 242-8049

Pat Busselle, Administrator
Commissioners Office
New Hampshire Department of Education
101 Pleasant Street
Concord, NH 03301
(603) 271-3879

Ruth Chapman, President
Ohio Alternative Education Organization
1512 Woodward Avenue
Springfield, OH 45506-2733

Dr. Ivan Cotman, Director
Enrichment and Community Services
Michigan Department of Education
PO Box 30008
Lansing, MI 48909
(517) 373-3260

Dan Daly, President
Minnesota Association of Alternative Programs
Moundsview ALC
4182 N. Lexington
Shoreview, MN 55126
(612) 482-8203

Dee Dickinson, CEO
Micki McKisson, President
New Horizons for Learning
PO Box 15329
Seattle, WA 98115
(206) 547-7936

Diane Duthie, President
Michigan Alternative Education Organization
Furmington Alternative Academy
3000 Thomas Street
Furmington, MI 48336
(313) 489-3827

Ray Eilenstine, President
Iowa Association of Alternative Education
University High School
1200 Market Street
Burlington, IA 52601
(319) 753-2701

Dean Frost, Director
Bureau of Student Services
Louisiana Department of Education
PO Box 94064
Baton Rouge, LA 70804-9064
(504) 342-3475

Robert C. Gaiser, President
Connecticut Association of Alternative Schools
185 E. Main Street
Branford, CT 06405
(203) 488-7291

Larry Garcia
Nontraditional School Accountability
Texas Education Agency
1701 N. Congress Avenue
Austin, TX 78701
(512) 463-7915

Steve Gargiulo, President
Alternative Education Association of Maine
340 Foreside Road
Falmouth, ME 04105
(207) 781-5013

Janie Gates, LeARN President
LACOE-ECE 126
9300 E. Imperial Highway
Downey, CA 90242-2813
(310) 922-6482

Becki Haglund-Smith, President
Oregon Association for Alternatives in Education
PO Box 69486
Portland, OR 97201
(503) 325-0910
(503) 325-6522

Gene Johnson, Coordinator
State Alternative Program/Learner Options
872 Capitol Square Blvd.
550 Cedar Street
St. Paul, MN 55101
(612) 296-6105

Al Koshiyama
Division of Adult Education, Alternative Education, and Safe
   Schools
California Department of Education
560 "J" Street
Sacramento, CA 95814
(916) 323-0544

Wally Lau, President
Hawaii Association of Alternative Education Services
Kapelema Heights
Honolulu, HI 96817

Dave Lehman, President
New York State Alternative Education Association
Alternative Community School
111 Chestnut Street
Ithaca, NY 14850
(607) 274-2183

Kelly Lyles, President
Florida Association of Alternative School Educators
419 Deunedin Circle
Temple Terrace, FL 33617-7801
(813) 985-7145
(813) 988-1880

Ronald Meade, Education Associate, School Climate and
    Discipline
Department of Public Instruction
PO Box 1402
Townsend Building
Dover, DE 19903
(302) 739-4676
[SDE - (302) 739-4601]

Deborah Menkart, Director
Network of Educators on the Americas
PO Box 73038
Washington, DC 20056-3038
(202) 806-7277

Al Meyers
Pennsylvania Department of Education
Office of School Services
333 Market Street
Harrisburg, PA 17126-0333
(717) 787-4860

Jerry Mintz, Director
Alternative Education Resource Organization (AERO)
417 Roslyn Road
Roslyn Heights, NY 11577
(516) 621-2195

Ray Morley
Department of Education
Grimes State Office Building
Des Moines, IA 50319-0146
(515) 281-3966

Ed Nagel, Office Manager
National Coalition of Alternative Community Schools
PO Box 15036
Santa Fe, NM 87506
(505) 474-4312

National Center for Restructuring Education (NCREST)
Teachers College
525 W. 120th Street
PO Box 110
New York, NY 10027
(212) 678-3432

Ken Payne
Virginia Alternative Education Association
PO Box 310
Monroe, VA 24574
(804) 929-6931

Karen Prickett
Alternative Education Programs
Wisconsin Department of Public Instruction
PO Box 7841
Madison, WI 53707-7841
(608) 267-9273

Elizabeth A. Quigley, Coordinator & Newsletter Editor
Pennsylvania Alternative Educators Association
Middle Earth, Inc.
299 Jacksonville Road
Warminster, PA 18974
(215) 443-0280

Carol Quimette, Director
Network of Progressive Educators
PO Box 6028
Evanston, IL 60202

Sheila Radford-Hill
Illinois State Board of Education
100 West Randolf, Suite 14-300
Chicago, IL 60601
(312) 814-1487

Dr. Mary Anne Raywid, Professor Emerita
Center for the Study of Educational Alternatives
Hofstra University
Hempstead, NY 11746
(516) 463-5766

Darlene Recce, President
Kansas Association of Alternative/Magnet Educators
1900 Hope
Topeka, KS 66604

Sally Roscoe, President
Colorado Options in Education
PO Box 1366
Frisco, CO 80443

Tyrone V. Seales, Coordinator
Virgin Islands Alternative Education Association
Department of Education
21,22,23 Hospital Street
Christiansted, St. Croix V.I. 00820

States Educational Alternatives League (SEAL)
1355 Pierce Butler
St. Paul, MN 55104
(612) 645-0200

Karen Vestigani, President
Alternative Education Association of New Jersey
PACE Alternative Education Program
1 Lincoln Avenue
Lake Hiawatha, NJ 07034
(210) 263-4344

Don Waldrip
Magnet Schools of America
PO Box 8152
The Woodlands, TX 77387
(281) 296-9813

Tom Wendt
CEC Alternative School
509 S. Dubuque Street
Iowa City, IA 52240
(319) 339-6809

Jack Wuest
Alternative Schools Network
1807 W. Sunnyside, Suite 1D
Chicago, IL 60640
(312) 728-4030

Appendix IV

Sample Alternative Schools and Programs

MONTESSORI PUBLIC SCHOOLS

Some well-recognized Montessori Public Schools are :

Bunche Elementary Montessori Program (AMS); PreK–5
(1991)
1111 Greene Street, Fort Wayne, IN 46803
(219) 425-7323

Charles Ellis Elementary School; K–5 (1927; 1988 Montessori
Magnet Program)
220 East 49th Street, Savannah, GA 31405
(912) 651-7357

Harold Holiday Senior Montessori School (1990)
  7201 Jackson, Kansas City, MO 64132
  (816) 418-1950

Henry L. Barger School; PreK–5
  (1954; 1993-Montessori program)
  4808 Brainard Rd., Chattanooga, TN 37411
  (423) 697-1224

George B. Dealey Montessori School (AMS); PreK–6 (1976)
  6501 Royal Lane, Dallas, TX 75230
  (214) 987-8525

Kennedy Elementary School, Montessori Magnet Program; K–5
  (1991)
  3800 Gibson Lane, Louisville, KY 40220
  (502) 485-8280

MacDowell Montessori School; PreK–5
  1705 West Highland Ave., Milwaukee, WI 53233
  (414) 933-0088

Mitchell Elementary School; ages 3–15 (1986)
  1350 East 3rd Ave., Denver, CO 80205;
  (303) 296-8412

Montessori International Early Childhood Education;
  ages 3–9 (1986)
  31 West Yale Loop, Irvine, CA 92714
  (714) 551-1647

Sands Montessori School (AMS); ages 3–12 (1975);
  first public Montessori in USA
  940 Poplar Street, Cincinnati, OH 45214
  (513) 357-4330

For more information, write *The Public School Montessorian*, a newsletter published by Jola Publications, 2933 North 2nd Street, Minneapolis, MN 55411; (612) 529-5001. Jola Publications also publishes a U.S. Montessori Community Directory.

OPEN SCHOOLS

The Brown School; K–12, magnet (1972)
      546 South 1st Street, Louisville, KY 40202
      (502) 485-8216

Metropolitan Learning Center; K–12,
      magnet liberal arts option (1968)
      2033 NW Glisan Street, Portland, OR 97209
      (503) 280-5737

Open Charter-Magnet School; K–5,
      individualized instruction focus (1977)
      6085 Airdrome Street, Los Angeles, CA 90035
      (213) 937-6249

Open High School; 9–12,
      community-based alternative education (1971)
      660 S. Pine Street, Richmond, VA 23220
      (804) 780-4661

St. Paul Open School; K–12, magnet school (1971)
      90 Western Avenue South, St. Paul, MN 55102
      (612) 293-8670

Steller Secondary School; 7–12,
      child-centered, humanistic, open learning environment
      (1974)
      2508 Blueberry, Anchorage, AK 99503
      (907) 279-2541

CONTINUOUS PROGRESS/MULTI-GRADE SCHOOLS

The Center School; 5–8 (1982)
>Community School District #3, 300 West 96th Street, New York, NY 10025
>(212) 678-2935

Central Park East Secondary School; 7–12 (1985)
>1573 Madison Ave., New York, NY 10629
>(212) 860-5871

Expo for Excellence Elementary Magnet School; K–6
>540 Warwick Street, St. Paul, MN 55116
>(612) 290-8384

Franklin Elementary School; K–5 (1980)
>2505 South Washington Street, Port Angeles, WA 98362
>(360) 457-9111

Garfield Elementary School; K–6,
>(multi-age program started in 1994)
>1914 Broadway Avenue, Boise, ID 83706
>(208) 338-3445

Jefferson County Open School; PreK–12 (1971)
>7655 West 10th Avenue, Lakewood, CO 80215
>(303) 982-7045

Wheeler Elementary; K–5
>5410 Cynthia Drive, Louisville, KY 40232
>(502) 485-8349

TRADITIONAL/FUNDAMENTAL SCHOOLS

Audubon Middle School; 6–8 (1959)
>3300 South 39th Street, Milwaukee, WI 53215
>(414) 647-0300

Barret Traditional Middle School; 6–8 (1986)
  2561 Grinstead Drive, Louisville, KY 40206
  (502) 485-8207

Butler Traditional High School; 9–12, college preparatory curriculum (1988)
  2222 Crums Lane, Louisville, KY 40216
  (502) 485-8220

Greathouse/Shyrock Traditional Elementary School; K–5, traditional elementary magnet and health promotion school of excellence (1979)
  2700 Browns Lane, Louisville, KY 40220
  (502) 485-8259

Kilmer Academy "5 R's Plus"; K–5, back to basics (1992)
  3421 N. Keystone Avenue, Indianapolis, IN 46218
  (317) 226-4269

Louisville Male Traditional High School; 9–12 (1977)
  4409 Preston Highway, Louisville, KY 40213
  (502) 485-8292

Milburn T. Maupin Elementary School; K–5, traditional instructional concepts in a comprehensive program and an advanced program in English as a Second Language (1993)
  1309 Catalpa Street, Louisville, KY 40211
  (502) 485-8310

Milwaukee Village School; 6–7, adding an additional grade level each year until grades 6–12 are included (1995)
  1011 West Center Street, Milwaukee, WI 53212
  (414) 265-2709

Whittier Elementary School; K–5 (1946)
  4382 South 3rd Street, Milwaukee, WI 53207
  (414) 482-3620

SELF-DIRECTED LEARNING SCHOOLS

Brown School; 1–12, self-directed learning magnet (1972)
546 S. 1st Street, Louisville, KY 40202
(502) 485-8216

Center for Inquiry; K–5, option magnet (1992)
6550 East 42nd Street, Indianapolis, IN 46226
(317) 226-4292

Hudson's Bay High School; 9–12; "Eagle's Wing" (1993)
1206 East Reserve Street, Vancouver, WA 98661
(360) 737-7368 for Eagle's Wing program
(360) 696-7221 main school number

Off Campus High School; 9–12 (1970)
14200 Southeast 13th Place, Bellevue, WA 98007
(206) 455-6183

New Orleans Free School; K–8 (1971)
3601 Camp Street, New Orleans, LA 70115
(504) 896-4065

Pan Terra High School; 9–12 (1976)
2800 Stapleton Road, Vancouver, WA 98661
(360) 696-7288

WALDORF SCHOOLS

Denver Waldorf School; K–11 (1974)
735 East Florida Ave., Denver, CO 80210
(303) 777-0531

Sacramento Waldorf School; K–12 (1959)
3750 Bannister Road, Fair Oaks, CA 95628
(916) 961-3900

Urban Waldorf Program; K–5, "public Waldorf" school (1991)
2023 N. 25th Street, Milwaukee, WI 53205
(414) 933-4400

Vancouver Waldorf School; K–12 (1971)
    2725 St. Christopher's Road,
    North Vancouver, B.C., V7K2B6
    (604) 985-7435

Information and a directory can be obtained from the Association of Waldorf Schools of North America (AWSNA), 3911 Bannister Road, Fair Oaks, CA 95628; (916) 961-0937, or from the Waldorf Kindergarten Association, 9500 Brunett Avenue, Silver Spring, MD 20901, (301) 699-9058.

U.S. Waldorf Teacher Education Centers are:

Antioch/New England Waldorf Teacher Training Program
    Roxbury Street, Keene, NH 03431
    (603) 357-3122

Rudolph Steiner College
    9200 Fair Oaks Blvd., Fair Oaks, CA 95628
    (916) 961-8727

Waldorf Institute of Southern California
    17100 Superior Street, Northridge, CA 91325
    (818) 349-1394

Waldorf Institute of Sunbridge College
    260 Hungry Hollow Road, Chestnut Ridge, NY 10977
    (914) 425-0055

PAIDEIA SCHOOLS

Albany Park Multicultural Academy; 7–8
    5039 N. Kimball, Chicago, IL 60625
    (312) 534-5108

Chattanooga School for Arts and Science; K–12
    865 E. Third Street, Chattanooga, TN 37403
    (423) 757-4835 elementary program
    (423) 757-5495 secondary program

Chattanooga School for Liberal Arts; K–8,
  "feeds" Chattanooga School for Arts and Science
  6579 East Brainard Road, Chattanooga, TN 37421
  (423) 855-2670

Eastwood Paideia Elementary School; K–6 (1990)
  5030 Duck Creek Road, Cincinnati, OH 45227
  (513) 533-6581

Shroder Paideia Middle School; 7–8 (1986)
  3500 Lumford Place, Cincinnati, OH 45213
  (513) 458-2040

SCHOOLS WITH A FOCUS ON MULTIPLE INTELLIGENCES

Contemporary Academy at Lincoln Middle School; 6–8 (1993)
  1701 Castle Avenue, Cleveland, OH 44113
  (216) 241-7440

Key Elementary School; K–5, school within a school (1987) at
  Washington Irving School #14
  1250 East Market Street, Indianapolis, IN 46202
  (317) 226-4992

Key Renaissance Middle School; 6–8 (1993)
  222 East Ohio Street, Indianapolis, IN 46204
  (317) 226-4992

SCHOOLS FOR PERFORMING ARTS

Hollywood High School; 9–12, performing arts (1903)
  1521 North Highland Avenue, Hollywood, CA 90028
  (213) 461-7139

Jefferson High School; 9–12, performing arts, television production, health sciences, biotechnology (1909)
  5210 North Kerby Avenue, Portland, OR 97217
  (503) 916-5180

New York City Public School Repertory Company; 9–12; (1992)
123 West 43rd Street, New York, NY 10036
(212) 382-1875

Pine Forest Elementary School; K–5, performing arts (1960)
3929 Grandt Road, Jacksonville, FL 32207
(904) 346-5600

Professional Performing Arts School; 6–12; (1991)
328 West 48th Street, New York, NY 10036
(212) 247-8652

School for Creative and Performing Arts; 4–12, fine arts (1974)
1310 Sycamore Street, Cincinnati, OH 45210
(513) 632-5900

SCHOOLS FOR MATH, SCIENCE, AND TECHNOLOGY

Cincinnati Academy of Math and Science; K–12 (1992)
2515 Clifton Avenue, Cincinnati, OH 45219
(513) 559-3000

Clemente Community Academy; 9–12, computers, math, science (1974)
1147 N. Western Avenue, Chicago, IL 60622
(312) 534-4000

Gladstone Academy; K–5, visual and performing arts, science, math (1990)
335 N. Elmwood, Kansas City, MO 64123
(816) 418-3950

High School for Engineering Professions; 9–12 (1975)
119 E. 39th Street, Houston, TX 77018
(713) 692-5947

Shawnee High School Magnet Career Academy; 9–12, aviation
technology
4018 W. Market St., Louisville, KY
(502) 473-8326

Western High School; 9–12, math/science/technology magnet
2501 Rochford Lane, Louisville, KY 40220
(504) 485-8344

ENVIRONMENTAL STUDIES SCHOOLS

Blanford Nature Center, John Ball Park Zoo School; 6, outdoor
education, research skills, independent study (1973)
1460 Laughlin NW, Grand Rapids, MI 49504
(616) 771-2555

Eagle Rock School; 9–12, service, outdoor education, environmental stewardship (1993)
Box 1770, Estes Park, CO 80517
(303) 588-0600

Lassiter Middle School; 6–8, environmental education, national demonstration site for the Center for Leadership and
School Reform
8200 Candleworth Drive, Louisville, KY 40220
(504) 485-8288

Multnomah Elementary; 1–5, interdisciplinary
academics/environmental issues and responsible
citizenship
2101 N. Indiana Ave., Los Angeles, CA 90032
(212) 223-2511

STATEWIDE RESIDENTIAL HIGH SCHOOLS

Louisiana School for Math, Science, and the Arts; 11–12 (1983)
715 College Avenue, Natchitoches, LA 71457
(318) 357-3173

Established by the state legislature, this was the nation's first public residential high school offering rigorous training in both academics and the arts. It is a state-supported residential high school founded to serve the academic and creative needs of gifted and high-achieving students. Enrollment is 400 juniors and seniors. No tuition, but room/board/fees equal about $945. Students can apply for fee reduction or exemption.

Maine School of Math and Science; 9–12 (1995)
75 High Street, Limestone, ME 04751
(207) 325-3303, (800) 325-4484

Maine School of Math and Science offers a residential alternative to high school students. The state also has approved a statewide residential high school for the performing arts to be initiated in the future. Its current enrollment is 164.

Mt. Edgecombe High School; 9–12 (1985)
1330 Seward Avenue, Sitka, AK 99835
(907) 966-2201

Mt. Edgecombe High School is a residential alternative school serving the state of Alaska. Originally a BIA boarding school for Alaska Natives, the school re-opened in 1985 as a statewide alternative. Serving more than 200 students, the school focuses on rigorous academic preparation, computer technology, and Pacific Rim studies.

North Carolina School of Science and Mathematics; 11–12 (1980)
PO Box 2418, Durham, NC 27715
(919) 286-3366

550 juniors and seniors; public, statewide magnet residential high school for academically talented juniors and seniors, established by the General Assembly of the State of North Carolina to provide challenging educational opportunities for boys and girls with interest and potential for high achievement in the sciences and math.

Texas Academy of Mathematics and Science at University of North Texas (UNT); 11–12 (1987)
PO Box 5307, Denton, TX 76203
(817) 565-4369

Tuition, books, and fees are paid by UNT; families are responsible for room and board and spending cash (financial aid is available). It was created in 1987 by the Texas legislature to provide an opportunity for talented students to complete their first two years of college while earning a high school diploma. Approximately 400 juniors and seniors attend.

TEEN PARENT SCHOOLS

Booth Memorial School; ages 12–20 (1929)
1617 N. 24th Street, Boise, ID 83701
(208) 343-3571

Comprehensive School-Age Parenting Program; grades 6–12 (1978)
Boston Public Schools at English High School
144 McBride Street, Jamaica Plain, MA 02130
(617) 524-4951

Lady Pitts School Age Parent Program; grades 6–12 (1966)
4920 W. Capital Drive, Milwaukee, WI 53216
(414) 464-9780

New Futures School; ages 12–21 (1970)
>> 5400 Cutler NE, Albuquerque, NM 87110
>> (505) 883-5680

Options Program; ages 12–21 (1984)
>> Hutchinson Career Center, Fairbanks North Star
>> Borough School District, Fairbanks, AK 99701
>> (907) 452-2000

Secondary Alternative School; grades 9–12 (1967)
>> 999-A Locust Street NE, Salem, OR 97303
>> (503) 399-3105

Stanton Alternative High School; ages 14–20 (1991)
>> 901 W. Whitman, Yakima, WA 98902
>> (509) 575-3489

DROPOUT AND DROPOUT PREVENTION SCHOOLS

Jefferson County High School; ages 16+
>> 4409 Preston Highway, Louisville, KY 40213
>> (502) 485-3173

Meridian Academy; 9–12 (1990)
>> 2311 E. Lanark, Meridian, ID 83642
>> (208) 887-4759

SAVE Program; ages 16+, grades 10–12
>> 410 East 56th Avenue, Anchorage, AK 99519
>> (907) 561-1155

Seattle Alternative High School-Sharples; ages 13–21 (1983)
>> 3928 S. Graham, Seattle, WA 98118
>> (206) 281-6916

Vocational Village High School; ages 16–21 (1968)
>> 8020 NE Tillamook, Portland, OR 97213
>> (503) 280-5747

Westbridge Academy; 7–12 (1969)
    615 Turner N.W., Grand Rapids, MI 49504
    (616) 771-3242

SCHOOLS WITH AN ACADEMIC/CAREER EMPHASIS

Barton Elementary School; K–6, traditional, emphasizing
    guidance/career education
    5700 W. Green Tree Road, Milwaukee, WI 53223
    (414) 353-5535

Belvedere Middle School; 6–8, media communications
    312 N. Record Avenue, Los Angeles, CA 90063
    (213) 266-3730

Central High School Magnet Career Academy; 9–12,
    medical allied health careers/medical office
    1130 W. Chestnut St., Louisville, KY
    (502) 473-8649

Crenshaw Teacher Training Academy; 9–12
    5010 11th Avenue, Los Angeles, CA 90063
    (213) 296-5370

Hawthorne School; K–5 (1989)
    4100 39th Avenue South, Seattle, WA 98118
    (206) 281-6664

High School for Health Professions; 9–12 (1972)
    at Texas Medical Center
    3100 Shenandoah, Houston, TX 77021
    (713) 741-2410

Marshall High School; 9–12, communications
    4141 N. 64th Street, Milwaukee, WI 53216
    (414) 461-8830

Port Houston Elementary; grade 6, international trade
    1800 McCarty, Houston, TX 77059
    (713) 672-0931

Skyline Career Development Center; 9–12 (1971)
    7777 Forney Road, Dallas, TX 75227
    (214) 388-5731

South Division High School; 9–12, tourism/food service/sports
    and recreation/hospitality management
    1515 W. Lapham Blvd., Milwaukee, WI 53204
    (414) 384-9900

Vocational Village High School; ages 16–21 (1968)
    8020 NE Tillamook, Portland, OR 97213
    (503) 280-5747

Wilson High School; 9–12, administration of justice and law
    4500 Multnomah Street, Los Angeles, CA 90032
    (213) 223-1131

EXPERIENTIAL LEARNING AND SCHOOLS WITHOUT WALLS

City and Middle High School; 9–12 (1974)
    Grand Rapids Public Schools, 504 College Road, Grand
    Rapids, MI 49503
    (616) 771-2380

Nova; 9–12 (1968)
    2410 E. Cherry, Seattle, WA 98122
    (206) 281-6363

Philadelphia Parkway Program; 9–12 (1969)
    4901 Chestnut Street, Philadelphia, PA 19139
    (215) 471-5007

Saturn School of Tomorrow; 4–8 (1989), state-of-the-art
learning technology, community-based learning
65 East Kellogg Street, St. Paul, MN 55101
(612) 293-5116

SCHOOLS WITHIN A SCHOOL

Accelerated Academy at Burbank Middle School; 6–8
Houston Independent School District
Houston, TX 77022
(713) 694-2813

Burke Academic High School; 9–12
244 President Street, Charleston, SC 29403
(803) 724-7290

Learning Unlimited at North Central High School; 9–12 (1976)
1801 East 86th Street, Indianapolis, IN 46240
(317) 259-5301

Step Program at Arlington High School; 9–12 (1976)
Arlington, MA 02174
(617) 641-1000

"CLUSTER" ALTERNATIVES

Central Park East Secondary School; 7–12 (1985)
1573 Madison Avenue, New York, NY 10029
(212) 860-8935

GEMS (Gardendale Elementary Magnet School); K–6 (1989)
301 Grove Blvd., Merritt Island, FL 32953
(407) 452-1411

Houston Independent School District Alternative District Office
3830 Richmond Avenue, Houston TX 99027
(20 cluster alternative high schools)

EXTENDED-DAY SCHOOLS

Burbank Elementary School; K–5
  3801 Underwood, Houston, TX 77025
  (713) 295-5230

Gilpin Elementary School; 1–5
  2949 California St., Denver, CO 82205
  (303) 297-0313

Logan Elementary School; 4–6
  2875 Ocean View Blvd., San Diego, CA 92113
  (619) 525-7440

Wilson Elementary School; K–5
  2100 Yupon, Houston, TX 77006
  (713) 523-9205

ALTERNATIVES IN COOPERATION WITH COMMUNITY COLLEGES

Atlantic County Alternative High School,
  Atlantic Community College
  5100 Black Horse Pike
  Mays Landing, NJ 08330
  (609) 343-5004

Blue Mountain Community College; high school
  completion/equivalency (1986)
  PO Box 100, Pendelton, OR 97801
  (541) 278-5804

Clackamas Community College; high school completion, vocational, teen parent program (1979)
  19600 S. Mollala Drive, Clackamas, OR 97045
  (503) 657-6958

Appendix V

Sample Charter Schools

ELEMENTARY LEVEL

Academy of Charter Schools; K–7
> 11285 Highline Drive, Northglenn, CA 80233

Bluffview Montessori; K–6
> 101 E. Wabasha, Winona, MN 55987

Canyon School; K–5
> 421 Entrada Drive, Santa Monica, CA 90402

Chinook Charter Elementary School; K–6
> 1472 Alderwood, Fairbanks, AK 99709
> (907) 474-4658

Core Knowledge Institute of Parker; K–6
> Castlerock, CO 80104

Darnall E-Campus; K–5
6020 Hughes Street, San Diego, CA 92115

Marquez School; K–5
16821 Marquez Avenue, Los Angeles, CA 90402

Metro Deaf; K–7
289 E. 5th Street, Suite 102, St. Paul, MN 55101

Northlane Math and Science Academy; ages 6–12
Freeland, MI
(517) 695-9909

The Open Charter School; K–5
6085 Airdrome Street, Los Angeles, CA 90035
(213) 937-6249

Palisades Elementary Charter School; K–5
800 Via De La Paz, Pacific Palisades, CA 90272

Vaughn Next Century Learning Center; K–6
13330 Vaughn Street, San Fernando, CA 91340

Yucca Mesa; K–6
PO Box 910, Yucca Valley, CA 92286

MIDDLE SCHOOL LEVEL

Community of Learners; 6–8
PO Box 4380, Durango, CO 81302

The Connect School; 6–8
24951 East Highway 50, Pueblo, CO 81006

Folsom Middle School; 7–8
500 Blue Ravine Road, Folsom, CA 95630

Jingletown Middle School
2506 Truman Avenue, Oakland, CA 94605

O'Farrell Community School; 6–8
    6130 Skyline Drive, San Diego, CA 92114
    (619) 263-3009

P.S. 1; ages 9–16
    901 Bannock, Denver, CO 80204

HIGH SCHOOL LEVEL

The Charter School of San Diego; 6–12
    3150 Rosecrane Street, Suite 200, San Diego, CA 92110

City Academy; ages 15–21
    St. Paul MN School District,
    1109 Margaret St., St. Paul, MN 55106

The EXCEL School; 6–12
    215 East Twelfth Street, Durango, CO 81301
    (970) 259-0203

Horizon Community High School; ages 14–19
    2550 Rogers Lane SW, Wyoming, MI 49509
    (616) 530-7535

International Studies Academy; 9–12
    693 Vermont Street, San Francisco, CA 90107

Lincoln High; 9–12
    1081 7th Street, Lincoln, CA 95648

Minnesota New Country School; 6–12
    PO Box 423, Henderson, MN 56044

Options for Youth; 7–12
    29 Foothill, La Placenta, CA 91214

Skills for Tomorrow; 9–12
    51 10th Street, South Dun 227, Minneapolis, MN
    55403-2001

GRADES K–8

Academy Charter School; K–7
>794A South Briscoe Street, Castle Rock, CO 80104

Cedar Riverside Community School
>1808 Riverside Avenue—Suite 206
>Minneapolis, MN 55454

The Discovery School
>Aurora Public Schools,
>18393 E. LaSalle Place, Aurora, CO 80013

Grass Valley Alternative
>10840 Gilmore Way, Grass Valley, CA 95945

Pioneer Primary/Pioneer Middle
>8810 14th Avenue, Stanford, CA 93230

Pueblo School for Arts and Sciences; K–9
>University of Southern Colorado
>2200 Bonforte Blvd., Pueblo, CO 81001

GRADES K–12

Charter 25
>6134 Highway 9, Felton, CA 95018

Community Involved School
>1829 Denver West Drive, #27, Golden, CO 80401

The Eel River School
>PO Box 218, Covelo, CA 95428

El Dorado Charter Community
>6767 Green Valley Road, Placerville, CA 95667

New Heights Schools, Inc.
>614 W. Mulberry, Stillwater, MN 55082

Parents Allied with Children and Teachers (PACT); PreK–12
    600 East Main Street/440 Pierce Street,
    Anoka, MN 55303

Toivola-Meadowlands
    7705 Western Avenue, P.O. Box 215
    Meadowlands, MN 55765

Appendix VI

Charter School Support Contacts

Jeanne Allen
Center for Education Reform
1001 Connecticut Avenue, NW, Suite 920
Washington, DC 20036
(202) 822-9000

Louann A. Bierlein
Louisiana Education Policy Research Center
Louisiana State University
111 Peabody
Baton Rouge, LA 70803
(504) 388-5006

Peter Birdsall
California Institute for School Improvement
1130 K Street, Suite 210
Sacramento, CA 95814
(916) 444-9335

Gary Cass, Supervisor of Public School Academy Program
Michigan Department of Education
PO. Box 30008
Lansing, MI 48909
(517) 373-4631

Charter School Strategies, Inc.
210 W. Grant Street, Suite 321
Minneapolis, MN 55403-2244
E-mail: CharterSSI@aol.com

Marcella R. Dianda
Southwest Regional Laboratories
Los Alamitos, CA 90720
(310) 598-7661

Emily Feistritzer
Educational Excellence Network of the Hudson Institute
223 N. Guadalupe Street, Suite 305
Santa Fe, NM 87501
(505) 989-4732

Kathy Haas, Administrator of Charter Schools
Arizona Department of Education
1535 W. Jefferson
Phoenix, AZ 85007
(602) 542-8264
[SDE - (602) 542-5393]

Scott Hamilton, Associate Commissioner for Charter Schools
Massachusetts Department of Education
1 Ashburton Place, Room 1403
Boston, MA 02108
(617) 727-0075
[SDE - (617) 388-3300]

Paul Hill
Institute for Public Policy and Management
324 Parrington Hall
University of Washington
PO Box 353060
Seattle, WA 98195-3060
(206) 543-0190

Institute for Policy Analysis and Research
819 Bancroft Way, Suite 100
Berkeley, CA 94710
(510) 843-8588

Ted Kolderie
Center for Policy Studies
59 W. 4th Street
St. Paul, MN 55102
(612) 224-9703

Alex Medlar
Education Commission of the States
707 17th Street, Suite 2700
Denver, CO 80202-3427
(303) 299-3635

Morrison Institute for Public Policysearch
Charter School of Public Affairs
Arizona State University
PO Box 874405
Tempe, AZ 85287
(602) 965-4525

Joe Nathan
Center for School Change
Humphrey Institute of Public Affairs
University of Minnesota
301 19th Avenue South
Minneapolis, MN 55455
(612) 626-1834

David Patterson
Regional Programs and Special Projects
California Department of Education
721 Capital Mall
Sacramento, CA 95814
(916) 657-5142

Pamela Riley
Pacific Research Institute
755 Sansome Street
San Francisco, CA 94111
(415) 989-0833

Don Shalvey
California Network of Educational Charters (CANEC)
San Carlos School District
826 Chestnut Street
San Carlos, CA 94070
(415) 508-7333

Society for Advancing Educational Research
57 Allan Close
Red Deer, Alberta, Canada T4R 1A4
(403) 340-0406

Bill Windler, Regional Representative for Charter Schools
Colorado Department of Education
201 E. Colfax Avenue
Denver, CO 80203
(303) 866-6631
[SDE - (303) 866-6600]

NEED MORE COPIES OR ADDITIONAL RESOURCES ON THIS TOPIC?

Need more copies of this book? Want your own copy? Need additional resources on this topic? If so, you can order additional materials by using this form or by calling us toll free at (800) 733-6786 or (812) 336-7700. Or you can order by FAX at (812) 336-7790, or visit our website at www.nesonline.com.

Title	Price*	Quantity	Total
How to Create Alternative, Magnet, and Charter Schools That Work	$ 24.95		
Beyond Piecemeal Improvements	23.95		
Creating the New American School	21.95		
How Smart Schools Get and Keep Community Support	24.95		
Parents Assuring Student Success	23.95		
Principal As Staff Developer	21.95		
Professional Learning Communities at Work	24.95		
Professional Learning Communities at Work video	495.00		
Building Successful Partnerships	18.95		
Adventure Education for the Classroom Community	89.00		
		SUBTOTAL	
		SHIPPING	
Please add 5% of order total. For orders outside the continental U.S., please add 7% of order total.			
		HANDLING	
Please add $3. For orders outside the continental U.S., please add $5.			
		TOTAL (U.S. funds)	

*Price subject to change without notice.

❏ Check enclosed   ❏ Purchase order enclosed
❏ Money order   ❏ VISA, MasterCard, Discover, or American Express (circle one)

Credit Card No._____ Exp. Date_____
Cardholder Signature _____

SHIP TO:
First Name_____ Last Name_____
Position _____
Institution Name_____
Address_____
City_____ State_____ ZIP_____
Phone_____ FAX_____
E-mail _____

National Educational Service
1252 Loesch Road
Bloomington, IN 47404-9107
(812) 336-7700 • (800) 733-6786 (toll-free number)
FAX (812) 336-7790
e-mail: nes@nesonline.com • www.nesonline.com